More praise for

How Women Rise

"A myth-busting 'how-to' for the next generation of women leaders and those who want to see them succeed. These ideas will transform our workplaces, our careers, and our lives."

—Rita McGrath, professor at Columbia Business School and a #1 *Thinkers50* Strategy Thinker

"Fast-forward your career with *one* powerful book from *two* of the world's most brilliant coaches. Marshall's famous strategies for behavior change combined with Sally's profound expertise on women will change your life from the first chapter. Start reading this book now!"

—Carol Evans, founder and president emeritus of Working Mother Media

"Women leaders will be driving forces in twenty-first-century organizations. Practically and persuasively, Sally and Marshall map out how this can and must happen."

—Stuart Crainer and Des Dearlove, founders of *Thinkers50*, the world's leading resource for identifying, ranking, and sharing extraordinary management thinking

"Pick up this book. Scan the twelve habits. Circle the top three that make you say, 'That's me!' Read those chapters, commit to one of the suggestions, and you're on your way. The authors know their material!"

—Beverly Kaye, founder of Career Systems International and co-author of *Love 'Em or Lose 'Em: Getting Good People to Stay*

"The habits and beliefs in *How Women Rise* provide a wonderful and positive opportunity for women to be self-aware. Sally and Marshall show women how to make tangible and crisp changes that will help them be even more successful and fulfilled at work and at home."

—Aicha Evans, senior vice president and chief strategy officer at Intel Corporation and a *Fortune* magazine Top Future Women Leader in America

"Women who seek to rise, take note! This is your essential go-to guide. Also highly recommended for men who work with, for, or around women."

—Liz Smith, CEO of Bloomin' Brands, the world leader in casual dining

"A gem and a revelation. If you lead women, work with women, are a woman, or know any women, you must read this book. Its sage and sane wisdom points the way to a life of genuine purpose and meaning."

—Richard Leider, international bestselling author of *The Power of Purpose, Repacking Your Bags,* and *Life Reimagined*

"When women approach the top of organizations, they can also bring their own strengths that may unfairly be seen as weaknesses. Sally's expertise and Marshall's wisdom bring these insights to light, so that women and men and can do better together at reaching their goals for us all to move forward. This is a powerful and timely book."

—Anthony Marx, president and CEO of the New York Public Library

"This is a must-read for women aiming to get to the next level in their careers."

—Michelle R. Clayman, founder and chief investment officer at New Amsterdam Partners and advisory council chair of the Michelle R. Clayman Institute for Gender Research at Stanford University

"The best leaders understand that in the shadow of their strengths lurk silent career killers. Sally and Marshall offer a brilliant lens to understand and transcend the habits that hold us back. If you want to lead at the top, *How Women Rise* is for you."

—Liz Wiseman, bestselling author of *Multipliers* and *Rookie Smarts*

"Whether you are just starting out in your career or a top executive, ample case studies, research, and wisdom make this engaging and actionable read a must-read!"

—Sanyin Siang, executive director of the Fuqua/Coach K Center on Leadership and Ethics at Duke University

"Sally and Marshall enable leaders who are women to move from *where they are* to *where they want to be* by sharing a blueprint for challenging the status quo and shining a light on leading change."

—Frances Hesselbein, winner of the Presidential Medal of Freedom, America's highest civilian honor

"The top 3 reasons why I loved Sally and Marshall's book *How Women Rise*? 1) It's incredibly helpful to women, those with female colleagues or direct reports, and the healthy minority of men who are also more self-effacing than aggrandizing. 2) The book is filled with news you can use. It has helped me and my C-level clients and will help you too. 3) The pages turn themselves. As a scientist as well as a coach, I can see the psychological and business sophistication behind the twelve habits. Start practicing today."

—Carol Kauffman, assistant professor at Harvard Medical School, and founder/executive director of Harvard's Institute of Coaching

"It's easy to find oneself in the pages of *How Women Rise*. Sally and Marshall teach us how to shift out of autopilot, jettison our success-inhibiting habits, and actively steer for the career destination we desire."

—Whitney Johnson, critically acclaimed author of *Disrupt Yourself*

"Compelling, practical, and highly engaging. Women seeking to make a career in law can benefit greatly from reading *How Women Rise*."

—Jami Wintz McKeon, chair of Morgan, Lewis & Bockius LLP

"Sally and Marshall's observations are brilliant—informed by both personal experience and deep scholarship. The behaviors they recommend are pragmatic and achievable; it is a book that will enhance women's effectiveness and ultimately their power."

—Anna Fels, MD, author of *Necessary Dreams: Ambition in Women's Changing Lives*

"Extraordinary real-life stories of women who wait to be asked to the party, get stuck in their comfort zone, seek perfection, and assume their hard work will be recognized. Sally and Marshall show us how to get unstuck and to 'stand out' so women can move forward in more purposeful, powerful, and productive careers. This is a must-read with great actionable advice!"

— **Janice Reals Ellig, CEO of Chadick Ellig and one of** *Business Week*'s **World's Most Influential Headhunters**

"Many of the behaviors most prized in women socially are exactly the same behaviors that hold them back professionally. But Sally and Marshall are here to help: identifying how and when to reconcile competing demands and motivators, without losing their identity, professionalism or power."

— **Margaret Heffernan, entrepreneur, CEO, and author of** *Willful Blindness*

"Sally and Marshall have written a practical and entertaining career guide tailored to help women ascend to senior leadership roles in business, government, and not-for-profits."

— **Geoff Smart, chairman and founder of ghSMART and bestselling author of** *Who* **and** *Power Score*

"*How Women Rise* is absolutely the right book at the right time by the ideal authors. Sally and Marshall's experiences and perspectives in leadership development, career success, and professional and personal satisfaction are each world-class in their own right. But taken together, they are magnificently complementary, creating an inspiring and actionable guide that will change the careers and lives of women leaders everywhere."

— **James M. Citrin, leader of Spencer Stuart's CEO practice and a member of the firm's Worldwide Board of Directors**

"I am broadly distributing *How Women Rise* to our leaders across Best Buy, to help our women leaders achieve their career goals and mentor their female colleagues, and to help men better work with and support the development of their female colleagues."

— **Hubert Joly, chairman and CEO, Best Buy**

HOW
WOMEN
RISE

**BREAK THE 12 HABITS
HOLDING YOU BACK
FROM YOUR NEXT RAISE,
PROMOTION, OR JOB**

Sally Helgesen and
Marshall Goldsmith

BOOKS

NEW YORK   BOSTON

Hachette Books
Hachette Book Group
1290 Avenue of the Americas, New York, NY 10104
hachettebooks.com
twitter.com/hachettebooks

First Edition: April 2018

Hachette Books is a division of Hachette Book Group, Inc. The Hachette Books name and logo are trademarks of Hachette Book Group, Inc.

The publisher is not responsible for websites (or their content) that are not owned by the publisher.

The Hachette Speakers Bureau provides a wide range of authors for speaking events. To find out more, go to www.hachettespeakersbureau.com or call (866) 376-6591.

Library of Congress Cataloging-in-Publication Data has been applied for.

ISBNs: 978-0-316-44012-7 (hardcover), 978-0-316-41822-5 (international trade paperback), 978-0-316-44010-3 (ebook)

Printed in the United States of America

LSC-C

10 9 8 7 6

Contents

Contents

PART III
Changing for the Better

We dedicate this book to Frances Hesselbein
Friend, mentor, hero

Authors' Note

The stories in this book are true, but names and some details have been changed.

PART I

On Being Stuck

CHAPTER 1

Where We're Coming From

In 2015, a mutual friend and colleague, Mike Dulworth, sent the two of us—Sally and Marshall—an e-mail with the subject line "Crazy Idea!" His suggestion? That we collaborate on the book you now hold in your hands.

We both immediately knew it was a great idea. Explaining why requires a bit of background.

In 2007, Marshall published his international best seller, *What Got You Here Won't Get You There: How Successful People Become Even More Successful*. There was a gold sticker on the front cover that read: *Discover the 20 Workplace Habits You Need to Break*. The lead endorsement came from Alan Mulally, then CEO of Ford Motor Company, CEO of the Year in the United States, and one of Marshall's superstar coaching clients: "Marshall's proven improvement process ROCKS!"

In the book, Marshall identified twenty behaviors that often trip up high achievers in their quest to make it to the next level. These are habits he's repeatedly observed hindering talented people from reaching their full potential, diminishing their ability to inspire and lead others, and at times even derailing their careers. The examples and stories were drawn from the global base of clients Marshall has developed over many decades as one of the world's most successful executive coaches.

A key insight in the book was spelled out in the title: the same behaviors that help people achieve high positions often undermine them as they seek to move further up. Because these behaviors worked in the past, people are reluctant to let go of them. On the contrary, many believe they are successful *because* of these bad habits.

Any human, in fact any animal, will tend to replicate behavior that is followed by positive reinforcement. The more successful we become, the more positive reinforcement we get. We can easily fall into the "superstition trap," which is: "I behave this way, I am successful—therefore I must be successful because I behave this way."

Wrong!

We are all successful *because of* the fact that we do many things right and *in spite of* the fact that we are doing some things that actually work against us.

Marshall wrote the book for a broad audience—not just leaders at the top of their organization's pyramid or ladder, but those on the middle rungs as well. *What Got You Here* is basically for anyone whose behavior gets in the way of where he or she ultimately wants to go.

Since publication, Marshall has traveled the world sharing and developing the ideas he put forth in the book. But in the course of doing so, and especially while delivering a series of workshops for women based on his 2015 best seller *Triggers*, he came to recognize that some of the more aggressive and self-centered behaviors he identifies as problematic in *What Got You Here* are less likely to be stumbling blocks for successful women than they are for men.

For example, instead of claiming credit they don't deserve, women are often reluctant to claim their own achievements. Instead of always needing to be right, women are more likely to be hobbled by the desire to please or the need to be perfect. Instead of refusing to express regret, women often can't stop apologizing, even for things that are not their fault.

Everyone has self-limiting behaviors, for the simple reason that we are all human. But although men and women do sometimes share the same undermining habits, they frequently do not. Women often face very different challenges as they seek to advance in their careers and operate on a bigger playing field, so it makes sense that women would adapt their behavior in different ways. And women are often rewarded differently, as we will show in the next chapter. These differences shape their expectations of what behaviors will be effective.

Given that Marshall's coaching base is typically about 80 percent male, it's not surprising that the original habits in *What Got You Here* would be those that most often hold back high-performing men. Marshall didn't view these behaviors as particularly male when he wrote the book, but rather as common forms of self-sabotage that could be corrected using the insights and practices he'd developed as a coach. Yet the more he worked with women, the more Marshall saw that they could benefit from a similar approach that addressed different behaviors.

Enter Sally.

Sally has been working with, writing about, and researching women leaders since the publication of *The Female Advantage: Women's Ways of Leadership* in 1990. Because it was the first book to focus on what women had to contribute to organizations rather than how they needed to change and adapt, companies began asking her to develop and deliver women's leadership programs almost from the start.

As a result, Sally has spent nearly three decades helping

remarkable women around the world grow their leadership skills and consulting with executive teams seeking to retain talented women. She has worked with some of the most successful women leaders in the world. This has given her both up-close exposure to the challenges women face as well as plenty of opportunities to observe what gets in their way.

The two of us knew each other well from the Learning Network, a small group for top leadership professionals that Marshall had started in 1996. But neither of us had considered collaborating on a book about behaviors that hold women back until that e-mail with the tagline *crazy idea*.

Because of our complementary experiences and long-standing friendship, we felt confident that by combining forces we could provide specific, helpful, and targeted guidance for women seeking to advance to the next stage in their careers and heighten their ability to have a positive impact—on their organizations, their communities, and on the world. Sally viewed the collaboration as a chance to help women address stumbling blocks that had held them back for decades. And Marshall saw a whole new world of habits that the coaching insights and practices he'd been honing for thirty years could help address.

We had also each had aha moments that confirmed our belief that women could benefit from a book on behaviors that get in their way as they seek to rise. These personal experiences have made us passionate about the need for this book and convinced us of its potential value.

Marshall's aha came while coaching the legendary leader Frances Hesselbein, who had coincidentally been extensively profiled in Sally's best seller, *The Female Advantage*. Frances will be mentioned quite a bit in this book.

During her long tenure as CEO of the Girl Scouts of the USA,

Frances had gained international attention when no less an expert than Peter Drucker, the founder of modern management, wrote that she was possibly the finest leader he'd ever met and suggested she be considered to head up General Motors. Upon retiring from the Girl Scouts, Frances assumed the presidency of the Peter F. Drucker Foundation for Non-Profit Management, later known as the Leader to Leader Institute.

Frances has earned respect and kudos from corporate, military, and nonprofit leaders around the world throughout her extraordinarily long career, and received almost countless accolades. She has twenty-three honorary PhDs, was profiled on the cover of *BusinessWeek*, and received the Presidential Medal of Freedom, the highest honor accorded to American civilians. Marshall was honored to accompany her to the White House when she accepted this well-deserved recognition from President Clinton.

Marshall had first met her when she was still with the Girl Scouts. He was doing volunteer work for the Red Cross, whose CEO at the time was a member of Frances's board and a mutual friend. When Marshall described to her the 360-degree feedback process he had developed to help clients become better leaders, Frances decided she could benefit from some coaching, and Marshall donated his time. As part of the process, he interviewed her board members, direct reports, and other stakeholders and wrote up a full report.

Not surprisingly, the feedback for Frances was incredibly positive. However, when she saw it, her immediate response was, "I have so many things I need to improve!" She then began listing about twenty-seven things she wanted to get right to work on. While Marshall was impressed by her dedication, he was surprised that a person of her stature was so self-critical.

He knew that most of the high-performing men he worked

with would have viewed the kind of feedback Frances received as a testament to their brilliance as leaders, as well as confirmation that they had little—or perhaps no—need to change. He was, unfortunately, aware of too many men who responded to negative 360 results by saying, "If I'm so terrible, why am I the most successful guy here?" or "I made five million bucks last year—and you're telling me I need to change?"

By contrast, Marshall recognized that his primary challenge in coaching Frances would be convincing her not to be so self-critical. In the years since, he's found this to be true with other fantastic women leaders. No matter how effective they've been or how much recognition they've received, women often tend to focus on all the ways they believe they fall short. As a result, when coaching women, Marshall usually starts with a ground-rule request: *Please do not be too hard on yourself.*

So Marshall's aha was that successful women's tendency to critique themselves instead of others opens them to different behavioral habits than men, who are more likely to accept recognition and deflect blame.

Sally's aha was more personal and painful, providing insight into a behavior that had helped her earlier in her career but was now getting in her way. By chance, it occurred when she and Marshall were co-delivering a half-day seminar for female engineers in Rhode Island.

Sally's usual practice before big events was to spend huge amounts of time rehearsing her program and memorizing her talking points so she could deliver her program smoothly and avoid any mistakes. So she arrived in Providence early on the day before the event and stayed in her hotel room to prepare. Marshall arrived late, so they agreed to meet on the morning of the event when the client picked them up in the lobby.

When the client arrived, Marshall (wearing cut-off jeans) immediately announced that he'd forgotten his pants, and asked to stop at a mall en route to the venue so he could buy some khakis. The client obliged, and as they drove around, Sally marveled at how Marshall seemed to be taking the incident in stride. For her, showing up for an engagement without pants would have felt like a literal nightmare, given that she often had anxious dreams of finding herself onstage half-dressed. But Marshall took the attitude that, since he travels a lot, stuff happens.

At the venue, where three hundred women were waiting, the only men's room displayed a Ladies sign and was awkwardly situated at the front of the hall where everyone could see it. Marshall paid a visit, but as he exited, he slammed his head on the inside purse hook (he wasn't used to one of these in the restroom) and tumbled out onto the floor. As he picked himself up, laughing, Sally again could not stop thinking how mortified she would have been if she'd made such an entrance.

As the day proceeded, Sally stuck with her tightly prepared program while Marshall took a fluid approach. Super-prepared, she felt an obligation to cover all her points and share everything she knew, while he engaged participants in spontaneous exercises.

An hour before the event's scheduled end, Marshall's pager beeped. He'd gotten his departure flight time wrong and now suddenly had to leave for the airport. He apologized but said he knew Sally would do a great job of winding up the program. Again, her first thought was how horrified she would be if she'd miscalculated her flight time. As Sally soldiered on, participants leapt to their feet to give Marshall a standing ovation. Some of the air went out of the room when he left.

Reflecting later on the experience, Sally realized that her exhaustive preparation and need to plow through every one of her prepared remarks had not served her particularly well. Diligence and a willingness to work extremely hard had helped her when she was starting out as a speaker, but contrasting her own dutifulness with Marshall's spontaneous and forgiving approach made clear that her audience would enjoy themselves more and probably learn more if she were less driven by her desire to be perfect.

Marshall had hardly been perfect. Yet the audience loved him, perhaps because his somewhat bumbling behavior was obviously authentic, and so gave them permission to be themselves. He not only articulated a message about the need to let go of mistakes, he *demonstrated* it in his behavior, showing how a highly engaged yet imperfect human could have an impact even when circumstances (the forgotten pants, the bathroom tumble, the misjudged flight) seemed to be working against him.

By contrast, Sally seemed to be demonstrating what being hard on yourself looked like.

You may have experienced similar aha moments when you suddenly see that behaviors that helped you get where you are now can hold you back from advancing to the next stage. Maybe, like Sally, you spend too much energy trying to be perfect, trying to please, or overvaluing expertise at the expense of relaxed communication. Maybe you struggle with speaking too much or too nervously or letting details undermine your focus. Maybe you find yourself hoping to be spontaneously noticed and rewarded for your hard work instead of advocating for yourself. Maybe you put your job before your career in an effort to demonstrate loyalty, or fail to enlist allies who can spread the word about your achievements.

If any of these behaviors are getting in your way, or you anticipate that they may do so as you move higher, please read on. This book is for you.

CHAPTER 2

Where You Are

Where are you right now in your work and your career? Are you in a place that feels satisfying and gives scope to your talents? Are you valued not just for your contributions but also for your potential? And do you feel your work is leading to a place that will satisfy your ambitions and help you make the difference you want to make in the world?

After all, you get to define what success means to you. You get to define what it means to rise. Maybe for you it's moving to a higher, more lucrative position. Maybe it's finding a wider playing field or getting more recognition for your work. Maybe you want more say in the direction your organization will take in the future. Perhaps you want to create a new business or product. Maybe you want to instill a spirit of joy among your collaborators, customers, and clients. Or you're fired by the desire to help other women get ahead.

The point is, your definition of rising is always going to be personal, individual to you. But one of the biggest impediments to rising is also personal and individual: being blind to the behaviors and habits that keep you stuck.

As noted in the previous chapter, these behaviors may have worked for you earlier in your career, which is why you may be tempted to cling to them. But as you move higher and assume more responsibility, what got you here—wherever you are now—can begin to work against you. This is true for men as well as women, but in our experience, the behaviors that undermine women are often different from the behaviors that undermine men.

Our focus on behaviors doesn't mean we seek to blame women who have not risen as quickly as they would have liked or that we don't appreciate the role external barriers play in keeping women stuck. Impenetrable old-boys' networks, sexist bosses, men who seem incapable of listening to women or who claim credit for their ideas in meetings, career tracks that assume families do not exist, performance review criteria subtly designed to favor men, the unconscious biases that shape hiring and promotion: these impediments are real and unfortunately continue to play a role in stymieing women's advancement.

Although women have made extraordinary and rapid progress in nearly every sector over the last thirty years, workplace structures and expectations created with men in mind continue to frustrate many women's talents and ambitions. So we repeat: we are not trying to gloss over or deny obstacles that we know are real. However, our primary focus in *this* book is not on identifying external barriers or providing road maps around them. It's on helping you recognize the behaviors that get in your way as you seek to become more successful on your own terms.

After all, your behaviors lie within your control, whereas external forces like unconscious bias may not. If the executive your boss reports to only feels comfortable talking with men he meets on the golf course, trying to change that will be an exercise in frustration. If your company uses performance criteria that subtly penalize women, you can be a voice for pointing this out and work with HR to explore alternatives, but it's difficult to persuade your company to immediately jettison how it evaluates performance.

However, uprooting an unhelpful habit, behavior, or attitude you've picked up over the course of your working life is the one thing that does lie within your control that can seriously improve your chances of success. At minimum, making the effort should improve your daily experience of work and better prepare you to reach your goals in the future.

So think of *How Women Rise* as giving you the means to clear your path of self-imposed obstacles so you can become more successful and take greater satisfaction in your work. Our goal is to help you make the biggest positive difference that *you* want to make on the path you choose through life.

HOW YOU DEFINE SUCCESS

Before we get started, we need to clarify what we mean when we talk about success, a word we'll be using quite a lot in this book. In our experience, women often define success a bit differently than men. This means they also define success differently than organizations have traditionally expected people (primarily men) to define success.

Instead of viewing money and position as the sole or even chief markers of success, women also tend to place a high value on the quality of their lives at work and the impact of their contributions. Enjoying co-workers and clients, having some degree of control over their time, and believing that their work makes a positive difference in the world are key motivators for many successful women.

This does not mean women don't care about financial reward or position—*not at all*. If women believe they are underpaid or feel their position in the organization doesn't reflect the level of their contribution, they will resent it. And this will certainly impact their commitment and their perception of success. After all, money and position are still the carrots companies use to reward people and recognize their value. And most of us work because we need or want money.

However, one reason organizations sometimes struggle to retain high-performing women is that they operate on the presumption that high salary and high position will always be sufficient motivators *even if the quality of work life is consistently low*. This assumption, especially when it comes to women, is often wrong. In fact, women are more likely to leave jobs that offer a high salary and position but a low quality of life. They often report finding such jobs "not worth it."

These are not wild generalizations. We are basing our observations on decades of experience, as well as on hard data.

For example, Sally and her colleague Julie Johnson joined with Harris Interactive, the polling company, to conduct a study of similarities and differences in how men and women perceive, define, and pursue satisfaction at work. The results appeared in their book, *The Female Vision: Women's Real Power at Work*.

The survey, which was delivered to 818 men and women who held management positions in companies with more than fifty employees, found many similarities between men and women. For example, both men and women reported deriving great satisfaction from leading teams, posting results that exceeded expectations, and being recognized for their contributions.

But the survey also indicated that men tended to place greater value on attaining a high position and earning a high salary, whereas women placed a higher value on the actual experience of work. Earning an excellent salary or achieving a top position did not feel as satisfying to women *if they were unable to also enjoy their days.* Not every day, of course. But enough to make the job feel worth it.

Men not only tended to view position and salary as more important than women do, they were more likely to judge themselves (and others) based on these measures. Sally and Marshall have both seen how this form of comparing can lead successful men to underinvest in key relationships, such as family, friends, and community, even though these relationships have consistently been shown to be essential components of human happiness and satisfaction.

Sally and Julie's research also found that men placed a greater value than women on winning, viewing it as a significant source of satisfaction and a key marker of success. They enjoyed besting competitors, "running up the score," and often assigned a numeric value or rank to their contributions and achievements. Women, by contrast, took less satisfaction in competition and scorekeeping and often went out of their way to describe winning as the result of a collaborative endeavor. Whereas men were more likely to describe themselves as "playing to win," women were more likely to agree with the statement "I will pick up the slack for others to assure that a project is successful."

Marshall's decades of experience working with successful leaders confirm these findings. When he was interviewed for the *Harvard Business Review,* he was asked, "What's the biggest challenge of the many successful leaders you have met?" His answer: "Winning too much!" As Alan Mulally, one of Marshall's heroes, observes, "For the great individual achiever, it is all about me. For the great leader, it is all about them."

The transition from achiever to leader can be particularly hard for highly competitive men, who may have difficulty recognizing that, as leader, their job is to make everyone else a winner. Women are less likely to struggle with this transition. Although many of the women Marshall and Sally have worked with like to win, they tend to be less interested in winning for themselves than in helping their organizations or their teams win.

This reluctance to view money, position, and winning as chief arbiters of success is psychologically healthy for women and great for their teams and organizations. But it can have a dark side, leading women to underinvest in their own success even as they devote time to building up others. This instinct for self-sacrifice also lies at the bottom of a number of behaviors that hold women back.

As you will see, the trick to maximizing your talents and opportunities is not becoming a less thoughtful and giving person, but rather being purposeful and intentional about your choices while also addressing the behaviors that keep you stuck.

THE PROBLEM WITH STUCKNESS

How do you know if you're stuck?

Stuckness usually manifests in different ways that are nevertheless interconnected.

- You feel something is preventing you from moving forward or from leading the life you're supposed to be living.
- You feel unable to break through circumstances that are conspiring to hold you down.
- You feel as if your contributions are not recognized or appreciated.

- You feel the people around you have no idea what you're capable of achieving.

Stuckness can seem circumstantial, the result of your situation or the fault of someone who has power or leverage over you. And this perception may reflect a degree of truth. But it's also helpful to consider the ways you might be keeping yourself stuck. After all, your responses help shape your circumstances. And your behaviors shape how others respond to you. That's why being able to identify these behaviors is so important.

Consider the following cases.

Case 1: Not being recognized for what you're good at

Ellen is a software engineer for a booming Silicon Valley company that has made a high-profile commitment to developing women. She's a talented engineer, but is also more outgoing, empathic, and socially skilled than many of her engineering colleagues. As a result, she's been able to build unusually broad connections during the three years she's been with her company.

She describes herself as "a go-to person," a fulcrum around which relationships form. Co-workers frequently e-mail her with queries or requests for help. She connects them with other employees who might be helpful or with resources they need. This helps her be effective in her job and improves workflow throughout her unit. Her boss has frequently commented on how well things seem to be going.

Because Ellen takes pride in her connectedness and sees it as an essential aspect of the value she provides, she was stunned when, during her unit's annual performance review retreat, her boss made the point in an otherwise excellent assessment that "she needs to get better known in the organization, have more of a presence, and more actively promote what our division is doing."

"I couldn't believe it," she says. "The very thing I've always thought I was best at, and he's telling me I fall short! He even makes it the center of his critique."

Having her efforts and skills go unacknowledged made Ellen feel unseen and undervalued, stuck in a thankless role working for an ungrateful boss. "I really felt hurt," she says. "How could he not recognize what I contribute?"

It wasn't until a few months after the review, when she heard a career coach talking about the need to actively bring attention to the value you provide, that Ellen realized what had happened.

"I saw there was a very simple reason he had overlooked my role as a connector: *I had never told him what I was doing.* I'd never mentioned all the people I connected with in the course of the day or the week or the month. I'd just somehow expected him to know. But he didn't monitor my e-mail, he didn't stand at my office door watching who came in and out, so he had no way of knowing how many people I was in touch with. I was actually bringing a lot of attention to what our division was doing, but I had completely neglected to let him know."

Ellen realized she had a problem with Habit 1, Reluctance to Claim Your Achievements, and Habit 2, Expecting Others to Spontaneously Notice and Reward Your Contributions.

Case 2: Keeping your head down before building alliances

Carrie recently got a big promotion in her financial services firm, heading the high-profile risk assessment unit. Having come from investment banking, she didn't have much familiarity with the extensive regulations that navigating risk requires, and felt a lot of pressure to get up to speed. The pressure was intensified by the fact that her predecessor, a former superstar in the firm, had made reckless decisions that resulted in government sanctions and was very publicly fired as a result.

Eager to help restore her company's good name and reward the executive team's faith in her abilities, Carrie decided to spend her first three months learning everything she could about risk management and studying regulatory requirements. She felt she needed to become an expert on the topic so she wouldn't make any missteps. Once she did, she told herself, she could come up for air and start building the relationships that would help rebuild her shattered unit.

But from almost the first day, she found herself inundated by requests for help and information she was not yet ready to respond to. The people in her unit wanted a clear sense of what she expected from them, and the corporate leadership team wanted to be kept informed. Carrie knew there were people in the company who could assist her, but she didn't want to ask for support until she felt she could speak credibly about risk. After all, *she* had been put in charge, which meant she was supposed to have a clear idea of what she was doing.

But Carrie's attempts to isolate herself in order to better understand her subject quickly earned her a reputation for being inaccessible and aloof. Her direct reports complained that she failed to give them guidance, while several members of the executive team feared she was withholding information as her predecessor did.

Finally the CEO, whom she'd known for almost twenty years, called her into his office and asked what the hell was going on. He said he'd put her in the job because people trusted her, but she was somehow managing to squander that trust.

Carrie was forced to recognize that she'd fallen victim to Habit 3, Overvaluing Expertise, as well as Habit 5, Failing to Enlist Allies from Day One.

Case 3: Overcommitting in an effort to please

Miranda is a senior associate in a thriving global law firm that has grown rapidly through a series of mergers. She regularly lands top assignments from the lead attorney who heads commercial law, her field of practice, and sees the potential to build a solid career in the firm. But she knows that in order to rise, she must be active on a few essential committees and get to know partners in the firm's widely dispersed offices.

So she jumped into the effort with both feet, volunteering for leadership positions in both the women's leadership network and the firm-wide network for native Chinese speakers. She also signed up for the committee planning the firm's global partners meeting, though it quickly became apparent that burying herself in details of invitation design, though it's something she enjoys and is good at, was hardly an efficient way to meet firm leaders.

Balancing these commitments with a sudden increase in the number of commercial cases going to trial proved challenging, but Miranda prides herself on being a glutton for work. So when a fellow senior associate in her practice recommended her to co-lead a new initiative examining recruiting practices in the firm, she leapt at the chance. The work required traveling to various offices to interview recruiting teams, which she figured would give her a chance to become more visible.

But her first trips made clear that she would mostly be meeting staff people to hash out administrative details rather than chatting up hiring partners as she'd envisioned. It was interesting work, but Miranda quickly realized she was being stretched to the breaking point. As her litigation practice heated up, she reluctantly decided to let go of the recruitment commitment, but worried that the colleague who recommended her would be disappointed.

She approached him with misgivings and was surprised when he quickly agreed that the project required a lot of work for uncertain rewards.

If that was so, she asked, why did he recommend her?

"Oh," he replied nonchalantly. "I was way too busy to do it. And you seemed like someone who would basically say yes."

Miranda realized that she'd been tripped up by Habit 8, The Disease to Please.

HABITS

Ellen, Carrie, and Miranda are all talented, hardworking, smart, and ambitious. They've chosen careers and companies in which they have the potential to rise. They've managed their personal lives in a way that has enabled them to advance in their careers. Each one of them is, in Sheryl Sandberg's great phrase, "leaning in."

But they've also let habits they developed at earlier stages in their careers get in the way of being able to move to the next level.

For example, Ellen's first engineering job was at a start-up led by a famously self-promotional lone wolf, where she benefited by never singing her own praises or talking up what she was doing. However, she now works in a very large company in which every division must compete for airtime. In these circumstances, her established practice of "not wasting" her boss's time by talking to him about what she's achieving ends up working to her disadvantage.

Similarly, Carrie's nose-to-the-grindstone approach won praise when she was an investment banker and was a chief reason she rose more quickly than her fellow trainees. But her new position requires leadership skills more than dogged work or subject matter expertise, which means she can't put off developing relationships or neglect those who look to her for guidance. She was chosen for her new position because of her reputation for integrity, not because she was an expert on risk. By not engaging people in her unit who have specialized knowledge, she signals that she has problems trusting others. This causes others to wonder what she has to hide.

Finally, Miranda's eagerness to please was viewed as loyalty and devotion during her early years at her firm. So the lesson she took away from her rapid promotion to senior associate was that saying yes is the way to get rewarded. This caused her to overlook the extent to which her commitments need to be strategic. By willingly volunteering for something that didn't really serve her interests, she allowed herself to be taken advantage of by a colleague who was sharply mindful of his own strategic path.

Each of these women, with the best of intentions, found a way to self-sabotage. Each played an unwitting role in her own stuckness. Each offers a great example of how extremely dedicated women can benefit by learning that *What Got You Here Won't Get You There.*

AUTOPILOT

In addition to feeling situational, stuckness can feel deeply embedded. As you become habituated to certain behaviors, you may start assuming they are intrinsic to your character, part of *who you are.*

So if you hang back from an opportunity because you dislike speaking before large crowds, you may rationalize that you've *always* been this way, even in grade school when you were among the last to raise your hand. If you're uncomfortable talking about your achievements during a performance review, you may recall that your mother always said that only selfish people talk about themselves.

This is why approaching change from a purely psychological perspective can be daunting. You have to work through all the layers and experiences that have habituated your responses. This is a time-consuming exercise that can be paralyzing and often requires professional guidance.

But approaching behavioral change by substituting new habits for old ones is empowering. It's also something you can do on your own, without help from a therapist or coach. After all, you probably have had experience tackling bad habits in the past. Maybe you smoked as a teenager. Maybe you used to munch on popcorn whenever you watched TV. Maybe you didn't really listen when people were talking but let your mind wander instead. Maybe you were always five (or ten or fifteen) minutes late.

As you discovered if you were able to overcome such habits, they were actually *not* aspects of your character. Nor were they reflections of "the real you." They were simply ways of showing up in the world to which you had grown accustomed, behaviors that had become your default mode.

Most habits get started for a reason. Maybe you were looking for a way to cope with stress. Maybe peer pressure was involved. Maybe you wanted to tune out situations that felt overwhelming.

The thing about habits is that they tend to hang around even when the conditions that got them started no longer exist. That's why spending a lot of time trying to figure out *why* you do them is usually not the most fruitful approach. You do them because you've done them repeatedly over time. They've become your go-to responses, unconscious and routine.

In other words, your habits are not you.

They are you on autopilot.

When you're on autopilot, you are not really thinking about *this* situation, *this* moment, *this* challenge, or the specific response it requires. You're just reacting in a way that has become comfortable for you over time. Your brain saves a lot of energy this way. You expend fewer mental calories. But you're not really present for what you are doing. Which is why you are not considering whether your behavior is serving you *now*.

It didn't occur to Ellen to give her boss the details about how she was connecting with people in the company because she'd gotten in the habit of not talking about herself. Keeping her head down had become her go-to response.

Carrie did not question her efforts to position herself as an expert in her new position because studying hard and mastering her subject was how she had always handled new challenges. She felt uncomfortable when she didn't know the answers.

Miranda never paused to consider whether saying yes to a colleague who made a suggestion would help get her where she wanted to go because she was so accustomed to saying yes. The word seemed to fly out of her mouth before she had a chance to consider the pros and cons of the suggestion.

Each of these women was using an old template in new circumstances, and managing to stay stuck in the process.

UNSTUCK

To get unstuck, to let go of a behavior that is no longer serving you, you need first of all to recognize it as a habit. You need to bring it to consciousness awareness so you can begin to try out new responses and see if these get you different results.

This can feel awkward and even dangerous. It can make you feel vulnerable, foolish, and exposed. But we have seen it work—hundreds, even thousands, of times over many decades. When it does, it unleashes energy and confidence. And that energy makes it easier to stay with the effort.

Ellen

Once Ellen got over her hurt and realized that her boss did not see her as a connector because *she* had failed to let him know, she was able to swing into action. She decided to e-mail him a brief note every Friday morning for three months listing all the people she'd talked to and noting how she had been able to help them. She didn't tell him what she was going to do or ask if she should do it. She just went ahead.

She says, "I felt pretty ridiculous at first. I kept thinking, he's busy, why should I keep bothering him to talk about myself? I felt self-serving, sucking up a lot of airtime to continually make the point about how connected I was. When I didn't hear back from him—which was usually—I wondered if he was sending me a message that this wasn't useful. But every once in a while, he'd shoot me an e-mail saying *good work!* And that kept me going."

At the end of the three months, Ellen and her boss had their quarterly meeting. As she entered his office, he came forward to greet her instead of remaining at his desk, as was his habit. "The first thing he said was how happy he was that I was letting him know who I was keeping in touch with. He said it was important; it was information he needed to know. He told me my connections were strengthening our team—which meant I was strengthening *him*. I'd never thought of it that way, but I realized it was true."

Carrie

Carrie's big wake-up came when her CEO confronted her about how she was losing people's trust. "I felt like resigning right then, or going off to hide in a hole. It killed me to think I'd let him— and the board!—down." Instead, she found the strength to suggest that she get him a few bullet points about how she planned to change—and get him those points by the next afternoon.

"I had no idea I was going to say that, but I knew it was the right response. He's a can-do guy with a short attention span so explaining *why* I'd gone wrong was beside the point. He would want action, which meant getting him clear, strong bullets immediately instead of a well-worked-out plan at the end of the month."

She started by jotting down everything that had gone wrong, not censoring herself, just letting it flow. As she read through her notes that evening, a couple of themes surfaced. She saw how frightened she was of not knowing answers to questions that in fact she had no way of knowing. And she saw how this fear had caused her to hide from the very people who could help her instead of enlisting them as allies in a common effort.

The bullets she sent to her CEO took the form of a targeted list of names: people in her unit with expertise in various forms of risk whose views and judgments she planned to solicit, sometimes singly, sometimes in a working group. "It felt uncomfortable, and a little late in the day, but I figured I had nothing to lose. If I went down, I would go down with my head up, asking my team what they thought, building relationships because that's what I'd been hired to do." It worked!

Miranda

Miranda was so shocked when her co-worker came right out and admitted he'd volunteered her for a thankless task because "you seem like the kind of person who would say yes" that she considered complaining to him or even telling her practice head. But then she realized he was only articulating something that was actually true. She *was* someone who could be counted on to say yes even when it did not really serve her interests. "I'm the one who put myself in that position because I'm such a people pleaser. Which means I'm the one who has the power to change it."

Although she felt awkward, she immediately let the hiring committee head know that her caseload made it impossible for her to continue with her volunteer role. Then she did something smart: she decided to practice a new behavior. She asked a good friend, who worked in a different part of her firm, to spend five minutes a day asking her to do things that she would then say no to. "I hardly knew what *no* felt like in my mouth," she explains. "I associated it with being uncooperative and self-centered. So I had to get comfortable with the idea that I could be a good person who could also be clear and say no when I needed to."

These sessions turned out to be so helpful and so much fun that Miranda and her friend decided to make them a regular practice, scheduling time to work on new behaviors and then holding each other accountable for making change.

Ellen, Carrie, and Miranda each discovered that changing specific behaviors could lead to changed outcomes: outcomes that increased the likelihood of their getting where they wanted to go. By recognizing the role they were playing in their own circumstances and identifying the specific behaviors that undermined them, they were able to make changes and get themselves unstuck.

CHAPTER 3

When Women Resist Change

So if you recognize that you need to change in order to move ahead, why is changing so hard? Because resistance is a powerful force. If you've ever struggled to stay on a diet, incorporate more exercise into your daily routine, become a more patient and engaged listener, or just be present for your moments instead of letting your mind constantly rush ahead, you know what it's like to battle the demon of resistance.

And make no mistake, resistance *is* a demon. It keeps you from having the life you want and imagine for yourself—at work, with your family, with friends, in regard to your health. That's why learning to recognize and work through your own resistance is one of the greatest favors you can do yourself.

Two factors are at play when you resist making changes you know could make a positive difference in your life.

First, there's the simple physiological fact that your entire neural system is designed to favor the path of least resistance, the path you've created by your prior thoughts and actions. When you repeat behaviors, you establish neural pathways, as if you're wearing grooves in your brain. This practically guarantees that you'll think or act in a similar way next time.

Those established pathways are the reason that changing familiar behaviors is an uncomfortable experience: basically, your brain tries to fight back. It sends urgent signals that you're missing familiar cues. *Hey, it's 3 p.m., why aren't you eating something sweet? Hey, that fragment running through your mind right now is more important than what the person you are talking with is saying. Hey, aren't you supposed to be feeling like a victim?*

Ignoring these signals requires neural energy and constant focus, which is especially hard when you're dealing with a lot of demands or trying to accomplish something. So you give in to the familiar signals (*okay, I'll just have half that doughnut*), even though doing so only strengthens the neural pathways that keep you bound to the habit you are trying to break.

Compounding the difficulty is the fact that you also invent rationales for continuing behaviors that have become comfortable or have served you in the past. If you reach for the sweet, you promise yourself you'll start dieting tomorrow. If you keep interrupting someone instead of listening, you tell yourself that they need to hear what you're saying. If you go down the self-pity rabbit hole, you wonder why the other person has chosen to attack you. All of this seems plausible until you consider that giving in to familiar signals today means they will be back to haunt you tomorrow. All you've done is given your established behaviors twenty-four hours to become more entrenched.

Successful people are particularly skillful at coming up with rationales to continue workplace behaviors that no longer serve them for the simple reason that these behaviors seem to have worked for them in the past. After all, they've received a few big promotions and gotten some excellent feedback over the years. They feel relatively on track. So if it's not broke, why try to fix it?

In *What Got You Here*, Marshall shows how resistance is often rooted in what he calls the success delusion—the belief that because you have been successful, not only do you not need to change, you probably should not change. Because if you do, you might lose your advantage.

As a coach, Marshall most often sees resistance to change manifest in three stages.

- In Stage One, the person decides that whoever is suggesting he needs to change must be confused.
- In Stage Two, the person begins to recognize that, while the general suggestion about change might be valid, the critique does not apply to *him*—if it did, why would he be so successful?
- In Stage Three, the person simply attacks whoever suggests he needs to change something about himself. He just blames the messenger. This enables him to continue buying into his own rationales.

Marshall has grown accustomed to seeing this pattern. But most leaders and powerful people are men. So the question we need to ask is *whether this pattern of resistance is also typical among women.*

Of course, some women react this way. Women, as we all know, are not all alike. Neither are men. Gender is only one factor in determining how each of us responds to feedback, observations, suggestions, and critiques—to any evidence that we might need to change a behavior.

That said, women often have very different experiences at work and may evoke different responses from those they work with. What they say is often heard differently, or not at all—a phenomenon popularly known as "speaking while female." They may carry more responsibilities, especially at home. They may define success differently, as we have seen.

So it's hardly surprising that women's resistance can surface in distinctive ways. Ways that can keep them stuck but that also give them a springboard for moving forward.

Let's go back to Ellen in the last chapter, the fast-track Silicon Valley engineer whose boss gave her low marks during her annual performance review because he didn't perceive her as well connected in the organization. His critique confused and upset her (Stage One in Marshall's original template). But she did not reject his observations out of hand based on the belief that she'd always been successful (Stage Two). Nor did she decide *he* was the one with the problem or blame him for what he had said (Stage Three).

No. Her emotional energy was engaged not in ramping herself into a defensive posture but rather in *feeling bad*. She was hurt rather than disdainful. Far from dismissing his assessment, she took it deeply to heart. If she hadn't conveyed what she was contributing, it must be *her* fault.

This response paralyzed her for a few weeks because she felt ashamed of not having lived up to her boss's expectations and a bit hopeless about being so misunderstood. It was only after she heard a career coach talking about the need to actively bring attention to the value you provide instead of expecting others to notice what you're doing that she began to ask herself *why* he had not accurately conveyed the value she was providing to her boss.

You'll note that, although she had enjoyed quite a bit of success in her short career, Ellen did not defensively focus on that in responding to her boss's critique evaluation. The stuckness she experienced did not come from any kind of success delusion, but rather from the inhibiting pain and sense of failure she felt upon hearing what he had to say.

Like Marshall's examples, her first response was resistance, but it was the resistance of *hurt*. Once she got past this feeling, she was able to move ahead rather than rationalizing, becoming defensive, blaming her boss, or concluding that she just couldn't cut it.

Both of us frequently see women who react to difficult feedback like Ellen did. So we've come up with three alternate stages of resistance to describe how women often respond to unwelcome feedback.

- In Stage One, a woman will react to the suggestion that she needs to change by feeling discouraged and undervalued. This can be quite painful and result in a degree of paralysis.
- In Stage Two, a woman will begin to consider *why* whoever offered the assessment might have made it. Were there valid grounds? What were the circumstances? Did the critique have to do with her being a woman?
- In Stage Three, a woman will start to examine how her own behavior may have played a role in shaping the perceptions that led to the critique. What might she have done or neglected to do? What might she do differently? Instead of focusing on the messenger, she looks at her own actions.

As you can see, resistance still operates in this model, but it takes a different form. And Stages Two and Three both offer a bridge to constructive action. They are potentially far more productive than Stages Two and Three in Marshall's model of what does not work.

Please note, we are not saying that women always follow this template. We have both worked with women who reject any critique out of hand and are highly skilled at blaming the messenger. But responding with hurt, so long as you can avoid feeling paralyzed or discouraged for too long, sets you on a different path that over time can actually yield positive results—if you can harness that hurt into action.

RESISTANCE AND STEREOTYPING

All of this is fine, you may be saying, but women still don't play on a level field, and this can affect how they are evaluated. To take a well-known example, research has shown that, when being considered for a promotion, women are most likely to be evaluated based on their *contributions*, while men are most likely to be evaluated based on their *potential*—nebulous criteria that can result in a less qualified man getting the job.

Stereotyping can also play a role in shaping the feedback women receive, leading to various "damned if you do, damned if you don't" scenarios. You speak too much or not enough. You are too aggressive or you fail to assert yourself. You smile all the time or you're always frowning.

So it's not surprising that the positive template of stages outlined above can become distorted. If you believe that whoever is offering you negative feedback is basically clueless about women, you're going to be less receptive to it. You may feel hurt—or irritated or amused or angry—but you're also likely to be skeptical and to consider the source.

A female investment banker Sally worked with in New York provides an example. "Our firm is famous all over the world for being dog-eat-dog," she noted. "Our people are ferociously ambitious and basically take the attitude, *I'm moving fast so you need to get out of my way.* Nevertheless, I was constantly critiqued by male bosses for having 'sharp elbows.' I always saw this as an example of unconscious bias. Everyone in our culture had sharp elbows, so it was basically a crock. I knew it, so I ignored the feedback."

Of course, men aren't the only ones who exhibit unconscious bias. Women can also be highly critical of one another. If you routinely receive negative assessments from a female boss, you may find yourself dismissing what she says based on your perception that she is hopelessly competitive with other women. Or you may have reason to believe she is jealous of you—because of the attention you receive, because you threaten her status as Queen Bee in a heavily male organization, because you're younger, or because of your looks.

Stereotypes can become particularly complicated when racial or ethnic differences get added to the mix. If you're African American, you may have good grounds for believing that your boss evaluates you using different criteria than he would use for white people. Or you may perceive that his communications with you feel stiff and inauthentic because he is only comfortable talking to people who look like him. As Marshall's client Kemala confided, "The head of our division was constantly telling me that 'my attitude' made people uncomfortable. But I think he said that because *he* felt awkward around me as a black person. He seemed to be projecting his discomfort onto others so he could somehow make it my fault and retain the image he had of himself as a great guy who could get along with all kinds of people."

After a bit of time stewing with resentment, Kemala decided to confront her boss in a direct but somewhat humorous way, presenting him with clippings that showed how common it was for African Americans to be criticized for having "an attitude problem." She then said she recognized she had room to improve and requested he be more specific in his feedback. "After that," she says, "our relationship began to change. He later told me how helpful my little intervention had been."

Similarly, if you're Latina, you may feel that stereotypes play a role when you get feedback about being "too emotional." If you're Asian, you may be suspicious when you're told you don't speak up enough. In either case, you may feel quite sure that these behaviors do not characterize you at all. And you may suspect that the feedback is based on unconscious bias.

You may be right about this, and if so, you might choose to confront it, as Marshall's client with the alleged "attitude problem" did. But it's also helpful to balance the recognition that stereotyping may be at work with a willingness to consider what role you might also be playing in creating a specific perception. If you find yourself *routinely* dismissing feedback because you believe it is biased, you might ask yourself if this could be some form of resistance.

After all, even if a degree of bias is involved, you are still being given information. It is important to remember that our key stakeholders' perceptions are real to them. Focusing only or even primarily on what's wrong with whoever gives the feedback is rarely the most effective route for reaching the next level of success. Instead, it can become a subtle form of blaming the messenger, which is a good way to keep yourself unproductively stuck.

One of the reasons Ellen the engineer was so successful in turning around her boss's perception was that she spent exactly zero time thinking about his potential faults. She worked in a unit of several thousand people, so she didn't really see her boss all that much. Almost all his direct reports were men, so he *may* have been uncomfortable with women—she really had no way of knowing. But she didn't focus on trying to find out. Once she'd gotten over her shock and hurt, she asked herself how her own behavior might be contributing to his evaluation and what she could do to change it.

In other words, she shifted her attention to what lay within her power. She put her energy into identifying what *she* could control.

As noted, biases are still alive and well in the workplace and can shade how women are seen and judged. But that doesn't mean feedback that might sound stereotyped has no validity or can't be helpful. Take the case of the "sharp elbows" investment banker. When Sally worked with her, she was about to make a transition to a high-profile government job that required significant diplomatic skills. The hard-charging manner she'd developed in banking would not serve her in this different culture. It had gotten her here but it would inhibit her rise going forward.

So she began listening more attentively to the feedback she received, asking for specific examples instead of dismissing it as absurd. "What I heard might have been sexist and probably was," she said. "But now that I needed to change, I also found it helpful."

OUR BELIEFS SHAPE OUR RESISTANCE

Trying to change a behavior that gets in your way rarely succeeds unless you understand the beliefs that inform it. Beliefs create the framework that shapes your actions. They provide rationales for how you behave and offer logical reasons for why you actually don't need to change.

In *What Got You Here*, Marshall identifies several pervasive beliefs that keep successful people stuck. These beliefs may have enabled them to achieve wonderful things. But these same beliefs can get in their way as they try to reach the next level or move to more challenging and satisfying terrain. These beliefs serve the cause of resistance.

A main theme running through the beliefs Marshall addresses is overconfidence, the belief that you have succeeded, will succeed, should succeed, and have the power to succeed by doing what you've always done. In his coaching practice, Marshall is very familiar with top executives whose unshakable (and at times delusional) belief in their own godlike self-efficacy and rightness can make them highly resistant to any kind of behavioral change. They view success as their due, the inevitable result of their hard work and strategic brilliance. In this schema, good fortune and other people play minor roles.

In some cases, such beliefs can actually be empowering. They spur those who hold them to take the big risks that are the hallmark of many wildly successful careers. They instill an optimism that others often find magnetic. They create resilience, the ability to weather setbacks and failures without giving way to paralyzing doubt.

Certainly, there are women who share these core beliefs,

women who rarely seem to question themselves, who walk into a room expecting to own it and view themselves as marked for success. But this is not always or even usually the case. Even high-achieving women often have to fight to maintain their confidence. They have to goad themselves into declaring what they're good at or remind themselves why they deserve a seat at the big table. They may read self-help books aimed at instilling confidence, or listen to inspirational audio books or podcasts while driving. They may practice positive affirmations, such as *I am bound to be successful in this endeavor!* They may act "as if" and try to fake it till they make it.

Even at the highest levels, overconfidence is rarely a major female failing.

Our experience suggests that there is a different set of core beliefs that often operate for women. These beliefs lie at the heart of their resistance, providing a rationale for behaviors that keep women stuck.

Belief 1: Ambition is a bad thing

High-profile women who seek to rise are routinely criticized as being "too ambitious." This is most notably true of female politicians. But it's also true of women in business, nonprofits, associations, education, or partnership firms who actively and openly seek their own advancement. You'll even hear the criticism leveled at women who are trying to position themselves to lead a volunteer effort.

What does "too ambitious" even mean? It seems to mean that any woman who is ambitious is unseemly, over-the-top, too nakedly self-interested to be trusted. Men are often described as ambitious, of course, but rarely with the qualifier *too*. It seems primarily to be reserved for ambitious women. So it's not surprising that even very successful women are often reluctant to describe themselves as ambitious.

The psychiatrist Anna Fels, who works with some of New York's top women in finance and law, noticed this reluctance when researching her wonderful book, *Necessary Dreams: Ambition in Women's Changing Lives*. So she asked some of her clients what associations came to mind when they thought about ambitious women. The most common words and phrases they used were *egotism*, *selfishness*, *self-aggrandizement*, and *the manipulation of others for one's own ends*. Given how they defined it, it's not surprising that even top achievers insisted to Fels that they were "just not ambitious."

Sally saw a similar reluctance when working with Nicki, a senior partner in one of the world's largest law practices. Now in her early forties, Nicki had joined her firm immediately after graduating near the top of her class at Harvard Law School. She was named partner a bit later in her career than some of her cohorts, but thanks to strong mentors and outstanding performance, she rose quickly into the senior ranks.

Despite literally being one of the most successful female lawyers on the planet, Nicki informed Sally within minutes of their meeting that she does not consider herself ambitious. "I'm driven, yes," she said, "but it's not the same. I think of ambition as being like a politician who knows from the time he's a kid what he wants to be, so he lives his entire life in that mold." She named a well-known U.S. senator who was a member of her Harvard class. "He was super-ambitious and acted like a politician from the day he arrived at school. Every relationship, every course, was chosen for the purpose of promoting his future career."

Nicki sees herself as very different. "I came to this firm because I thought it would be a great place to start my career, not because I saw myself as a partner. I ended up staying because I love the work and because I love the feedback I get for my work. I've always been motivated by good feedback. That's why I got good grades in school. It's the same here: I enjoy pleasing the client, the judge, or the partner in charge. That's basically been my motivation."

Clearly, Nicki views ambition through a negative lens. She doesn't want to be associated with the word, even though one might think that climbing to the top of a major global law firm would both require and give proof of ambition.

Nicki also associates ambition with being focused solely on positional power, which she says does not motivate her. "My work at the firm has never been about position. I'm here because I find the work satisfying and enjoy the challenge." Her attitude reflects the research cited in Chapter 2 showing that women tend to be more engaged by a high-quality work experience and the belief that they are having an impact than by abstract measures of position and rank.

Yet it's striking the extent to which women allow ambition to be defined for them. There's no reason that aspiring to have satisfying work and make a difference in the world cannot be a form of ambition, no reason ambition must automatically be viewed as arrogant, self-centered, or untrustworthy. Ambition might more usefully be defined as the desire to maximize your talents in the service of work you find worthwhile and rewarding. Choosing to believe otherwise, or making negative judgments about ambition, can become a way to rationalize resistance.

Belief 2: Being a good person means not disappointing others

Many women we work with are deeply invested in being wonderful people. This is a great thing and helps make the world a better place. But this desire can work against you if it is allied with the belief that being wonderful means never disappointing others. We already saw this with Miranda, the senior law firm associate who stuck with a time-consuming commitment that undermined her effectiveness because she was reluctant to disappoint a casual colleague. Even though that colleague had volunteered her for a role that *he* preferred to avoid.

Marshall worked with a consultant who was beloved throughout her firm and industry. She was known among colleagues and clients as "the wonderful Lina." Other firms had tried to hire her, but she refused to consider any offer because she did not want to break up her team. In part, this was savvy: she knew that she benefited from the work of those she had nurtured. She therefore did not imagine that what she had achieved could be duplicated in any circumstance simply because of her own brilliance, as many of her peers clearly believed about themselves.

Finally, a competing firm made an offer for Lina and her entire team, with a contract that gave her unprecedented latitude and support. She was thrilled, but when she approached her team, several members were reluctant to move for personal reasons. They also expressed disappointment that she would consider leaving a practice that had been so good to her.

This pushback was deeply upsetting to Lina. She began thinking about all the mentors, sponsors, and senior leaders in her firm who had gone out of their way for her over the years. How would they react to her leaving? Would they view her as ungrateful? And how could she still be "the wonderful Lina" if she not only bailed on her colleagues but took part of her team along with her?

After a lot of angst, she decided to turn down the offer. There were some good reasons for doing so. But her desire not to disappoint people in order to maintain her self-image as a wonderful person got in the way of her ability to objectively analyze the pros and cons of the offer. Her inability to separate her own interests from the expectations of others had become for her a form of resistance. Ultimately, Lina ended up regretting her decision when two of her most important team members left for better offers.

Belief 3: Women should always be role models for other women

Marissa Mayer was still CEO of Yahoo! when she became pregnant with twin girls. Although she had led a revamp of the company's parental leave policies to be far more generous, she announced that she herself would be taking limited time off for the births and working throughout.

Her decision caused a storm of protest, the primary criticism being that Mayer was failing to serve as a role model, not only for her own employees but, as one press commentator put it, "for women everywhere." Another critic lamented, "What kind of message does it send? She's really setting back what all women have worked for. When you're at her level, there's no such thing as a personal decision because other women are looking to you for guidance."

The idea that high-profile women do not get to make their own life choices without first considering the potential impact upon all other women is a pernicious trap. Being successful at a demanding job while trying to maintain a rewarding personal life is tough enough for anyone in today's demanding work culture. Expecting women to also calculate personal decisions based on how others will interpret them adds an extra burden. It's certainly not a burden men are expected to bear.

Yet women often find their decisions and setbacks scrutinized through the role model lens. This can become a source of shame and guilt, while also setting women against one another. The burden is particularly intense for minority women, who are often expected to carry the aspirations of not only other women, but their entire ethnic or racial group on their shoulders. If you find yourself bound by such expectations, it may be time to plot your escape from role model hell. Holding it as a core belief can undermine you. Which, when you think about it, doesn't do other women any favors.

The beliefs described above all have their root in society's expectation that women should put the needs of others ahead of their own. This expectation begins early. In general, girls are rewarded for being thoughtful and obedient while boys are given more latitude. Both men and women carry this legacy with them into the workplace. While altering societal attitudes will take decades, you can in the meantime benefit from considering whether you have internalized beliefs and expectations that seem almost designed to hold you back.

PART II

The Habits That Keep Women from Reaching Their Goals

CHAPTER 4

The Twelve Habits

The twelve habits presented in this book are behaviors we routinely observe getting in the way of successful women's efforts to rise.

Of course, not all of these behaviors apply to all women. Most women we have worked with struggle with only a few, while a few exhibit none. But decades of professional experience with women in virtually every sector have taught us that even women at the highest levels can undermine themselves with specific self-sabotaging behaviors that are different from those that most frequently undermine men.

This is not surprising. As noted in Chapter 3, habits and behaviors develop in response to experiences, and women often have different experiences in the workplace than men. This doesn't always show up during the first few years in a woman's work life. But at some point, these differences emerge... and over the years, they begin to take their toll.

Take that well-known phenomenon of "speaking while female." A range of studies confirms the truth of a common female perception: that men often have trouble hearing women when they speak. A typical example occurs in meetings where there are very few women present—or even only one, that one being you. You make a point or an observation during a discussion. No one comments or appears to notice. Other participants carry on with the conversation.

Then a man, often senior but not necessarily, makes the exact same point you just made. But the response this time is very different. "Great idea, Jack!" Or, "I agree with what Jack says." Or, "I just want to build on Jack's point."

Suddenly, Jack owns the insight.

You look around the room. Nobody seems to notice what just happened. So now you're in a quandary. Should you point out that Jack is echoing your observations? Should you try to claim credit for what you said? And why didn't anyone notice when *you* made the point?

If Jack is senior to you, you probably let it go. After all, organizations rarely look kindly on people who correct higher-ups, especially in front of others. And bosses typically receive credit for ideas that originate with the people who work for them. That's a fact of life in any hierarchical culture.

But what if Jack is a peer or holds a position a notch down the chain of command from you? You feel like a fool just sitting there and letting yourself be ignored. But might speaking up make you seem petty and aggrieved? Maybe you remember a female colleague who got slammed for making a similar objection in a previous meeting. Or you worry that Jack or one of his buddies might retaliate. Finally, you decide there's no sense making an enemy, so you keep your mouth shut. But the feeling that you've been disrespected stays with you, and it colors your interactions with Jack (and perhaps with other colleagues in that room) moving forward.

This is a common scenario; we hear variations on it all the time. It's one of those little pinpricks women routinely face throughout the course of their work lives. You'll find suggestions on how to handle this kind of situation in Chapters 13 and 14. What matters is that encounters like this often shape women's experience of work. And because experience shapes behavior, repeatedly having your voice ignored may begin to influence how you respond even when people are hanging on your every word.

And your responses, over time, become habits.

GENDER NEUTRAL

In *What Got You Here Won't Get You There*, Marshall examines twenty habits or behaviors he routinely sees getting in the way of successful people. Some of these, while common among the male executives who form his client base, tend to be less typical of women.

These behaviors include:

- Winning too much
- Telling the world how smart you are
- Claiming credit you don't deserve
- Failing to give others proper recognition
- Using anger as a management tool
- Refusing to express regret
- Failing to express gratitude
- Passing the buck

If you feel any of these behaviors are a problem for you, you will want to consult *What Got You Here* for ideas on how you might let go of them. But upon reflection, we just don't see these behaviors as being particularly problematic for most women. Sometimes yes, but not all that often.

Other habits described in Marshall's book tend to be more gender neutral. Let's take a brief look at four of these behaviors.

Passing judgment

If you hear yourself thinking, *Why does he say things like that? I never would!* you are passing judgment on that person.

Passing judgment means feeling the need to impose your standards on others, as if their job were to live up to your expectations. You don't have to do this verbally. You can also judge another person in your head, comparing his or her behavior to what *you* would do, usually in a way that shows you to be superior.

If you think about it, this is really futile.

Exactly *why* would you expect all the people you work with to have the same standards of behavior that you do? Just because you don't throw tantrums, plot revenge, or try to suck up all the oxygen in the room doesn't mean nobody else does. So there's no sense in being stunned because a colleague, boss, or client occasionally (or even often) behaves like a total jerk.

Marshall worked with a highly judgmental CEO who took delight in rating people's answers to questions he posed in meetings. "Great idea," he'd say to one volunteer. "Not so bad," to another. "Where'd you come up with that one?" to a third. When Marshall called him on it, he claimed he was just being helpful to his staff. But of course people viewed what he was doing as passing judgment. It had never occurred to him that it was better to listen instead of weigh in immediately with his responses, to let things unfold and take time to consider all he was being told. After learning this seemingly simple point, he made amazing progress in becoming a more effective listener.

Passing judgment is often the engine for the kind of gossipy conversations that can make a workplace toxic. It may feel satisfying to share negative views of co-workers you find difficult or believe are off track, but judgmental observations waste your time and create negative energy that saps your spirit and can alienate others.

Gossip also diminishes you as a leader since accepting others *with their flaws* is the first step toward figuring out how to deal with them effectively, which is precisely what good leaders do. The more clearly you see people, the more strategic you can be. Clouding your response with negative assessments can only get in your way.

Starting with no, but, or however

"No, we've already tried it that way, and we saw how *that* turned out."

"But what if that information doesn't come through as planned?"

"However, one thing you forgot to say was..."

You may habitually use negative qualifiers to start your sentences during meetings or performance reviews. You may even use them in brainstorming sessions, where the "no idea is a bad idea" rule is supposed to be in effect. You might not actually disagree with what others are saying. You might simply be teeing up your thoughts or trying to emphasize the importance of what you have to say. Or maybe you just say *no*, *but*, or *however* because you've gotten in the habit.

But starting with a negative qualifier always amounts to a direct contradiction of what someone else is saying. You may not mean it, but the person you are speaking with hears it this way. They hear, "Your point may be fine, but mine is better." Or, "Forget that, what I'm about to say really matters."

Negative qualifiers operate as verbal tics, habits of speech you may not even be aware of. It's always better to make your point without first disqualifying what the speaker before you said. A simple *yes*, *and*, or *thank you* makes a more gracious segue to what you have to add or say.

Making excuses

In *What Got You Here*, Marshall notes that people at work typically use two kinds of excuses, either blunt or subtle. Blunt excuses are of the "my dog ate my homework" variety: "Sorry I was late, my babysitter's car broke down." Or "Sorry I missed the meeting, my Google calendar malfunctioned."

The problem with blunt excuses is that they're an ineffective way of positioning yourself as a leader, as someone whom others can look to and trust. Resorting to them regularly makes you look as if you don't have your act together or don't want to take responsibility for your actions. An unadorned "I'm sorry" is always more effective.

Blunt excuses are particularly ineffective if you are also in the habit of apologizing for things that are not remotely your fault. You can read more about this behavior, which is more typical of women than men, in Chapter 13.

Subtle excuses are those you use to attribute a failing to some character flaw, as if it were a permanent and unalterable aspect of who you are. Both men and women often make subtle excuses, but the excuses women use often seem almost designed to put them in a poor light.

"I've always been a disorganized person."

"I don't seem able to keep my mouth shut."

"I'm easily hurt."

"I'm way too into people-pleasing—it's a terrible fault."

When you make such statements, you may feel as if you're assuming responsibility for your actions, but others hear you as suggesting that you're incapable of change. You never gain an advantage by stereotyping yourself in a negative manner. And you undercut your ability to let go of behaviors that hold you back if you cling to the self-defeating belief that they are somehow part of your genetic makeup.

An excessive need to be me

There's been a lot of emphasis on authenticity in the workplace in recent years. The idea often seems to be that honesty requires indulging your faults or proclaiming your shortcomings. This habit often proceeds from the assumption that trying to change your behavior would somehow be a betrayal of the real you.

Though an excessive "need to be me" is gender neutral, men and women often manifest it in different ways. Marshall hears senior male executives vehemently defending their unwillingness to praise people who work for them on the grounds that for them to do so would be phony. "That's not how I talk," they might say. "It wouldn't be authentic for me to gush over a subordinate's performance." Women caught in the authenticity trap are more likely to say things such as, "I'm just not the self-promotional type."

But if you know a behavior isn't working for you, and you persist on doing it anyway, that's not being authentic: that's just being stubborn.

So whenever you hear yourself proclaiming that something is *just not you*, you might want to question your motivation. An excessive devotion to a particular self-image can be a rationale for remaining stuck. It's a form of obstinacy that will get in your way as you seek to rise.

HOW ORGANIZATIONS MAKE IT HARD TO CHANGE BEHAVIORS

Our global economy stands still for no one, so one of the big challenges leaders face today is positioning their organizations to operate on the cutting edge. This means getting comfortable with a constantly shifting environment, which is why most organizations are so eager to tell you that they embrace and thrive on change.

Nevertheless, the cruel irony is that despite positioning themselves as change agents, organizations routinely if inadvertently make it difficult for the people *within* them to change. This is true for two reasons.

First, without really intending to, people in organizations often assign one another an identity or a role based on past behavior. For example:

- "Marcy would be a good choice for the task force; she's always eager to volunteer."

- "Someone other than Sandra should probably handle this job. It calls for diplomacy and tact, and she's always so blunt."
- "Chantal is a great listener—she'd be good in this role."

Of course, there's nothing wrong with taking people's skills and dispositions into account when handing out assignments. But it can have the effect of keeping people stuck in a rut. It shields them from challenges that could benefit their development, and denies them the chance to practice new behaviors. And should they try to break free from familiar patterns, they may stir blowback.

Say you're Marcy and you've begun to recognize that your eagerness to volunteer for extra assignments is rooted in a desire to please or placate others, even when doing so doesn't serve your best interests. You've decided to try to be more strategic in evaluating which opportunities to pursue and which to let pass. So when someone on your team asks for volunteers for a project that doesn't fit your strategic goals, you force yourself to sit on your hands.

You may feel pleased that you're showing discipline. But then a colleague expresses surprise that you aren't signing up. "You're always so helpful," she might say. Or, "What happened? You're usually first in line." The implication is that you've stepped out of character and disappointed expectations by departing from your usual script.

When this happens, you may feel pressured to act more "in character." The positive behavioral changes you're trying to make have run up against expectations that keep you trapped. A good solution in this situation is to tell the person who pushes back that you're working on a new behavior. You'll find plenty of suggestions for how to do this in Part III. The point here is that people in organizations often assign one another roles based on previous behavior, which has the effect of making it difficult to practice new ones.

The second way organizations make it hard for people to change is through their strong bias for action.

Almost every organization is designed to demonstrate a commitment to positive action, to *doing things*. "We are pursuing new markets in X." "We are expanding our offerings to include Y." "We are instituting a new accountability system." There is rarely any mention of paths not taken, actions not pursued. Even when deliberate inaction saves the organization a bundle, this is rarely discussed for the simple reason that inaction is not seen as a virtue.

And so at a team retreat, you may be told that focusing your attention on new-customer needs must be your top priority. But you will rarely be encouraged to stop checking your phone every few minutes so you can be more fully present for what your customer is saying. The emphasis is always on what you should do, never on what you should *stop* doing.

Similarly, your company's CEO might regularly give motivational "talks to the troops" in which he or she sings the praises of being a good team player. But how often do you hear leadership exhorting top performers to focus *less* on making their numbers in order to better support the team?

Because of this bias for action, organizations recognize and reward people primarily for what they do—bringing in a new client, signing a deal, hitting a number. Rarely is someone congratulated, much less rewarded, for avoiding a deal that could have gone wrong, even when the result would clearly have been catastrophic. Instead, those who raise warnings about the consequences of various actions are often viewed as naysayers, out of step in a can-do culture.

It may sound paradoxical that this bias for action could make it hard for people to change, since change is usually associated with taking action. If you want to get fit, you head for the gym. If you want to rise in the organization, you put in more hours. But a key insight as you progress in your career is that behavioral change is often about *not* acting rather than acting. As the business sage Peter Drucker famously noted, "We spend a lot of time teaching leaders what to do. We don't spend nearly enough time teaching them what to stop."

Marshall's decades of coaching confirm the wisdom of Drucker's remark. He finds that clients who make long lists of "to-do" behaviors (*say please and thank you, be more patient, treat others with respect*) have a more difficult time changing than those who focus on a few "must-stop" behaviors (*stop sharing your opinion on everything, quit taking other people's work for granted, don't claim credit you don't deserve*). Even the simple injunction to "stop being a jerk" is often more effective than itemizing desirable behaviors to try out.

Sally has also seen how the bias for action can undermine the ability of people to let go of behaviors that no longer serve them. A vivid example came during a recent client call about a leadership workshop she was scheduled to deliver. After she had sketched out the program, the head of the planning committee spoke up.

"The most important thing is that your program should be immediately actionable," she said. "We have a very proactive culture around here, so we want to make sure you give people plenty of to-dos. The ideal would be for participants to walk away with five new things they can do Monday morning."

Sally had heard such requests in the past and tried to accommodate them. But now she pushed back. She noted that in her experience the last thing most people in organizations need is five new things to do on Monday morning. With employees already overloaded, adding new items to already crowded to-do lists can be counterproductive. In addition, evaluations from Sally's programs showed that participants reported gaining the most value from having time and space to reflect on their priorities instead of adding new ones. She made that case, sharing data on past results, and persuaded the client to let her focus the workshop on helping participants be more effective and thoughtful rather than busier.

THE HABITS

So the focus of this book is not about *new* habits and behaviors you might want to start practicing, since we figure you probably already have enough to-do items on your list. Instead, our goal is to teach you about the "must-stop" habits that in our experience are most likely to get in your way as a woman. Habits that might once have served you but can undermine you as you seek to rise.

The twelve chapters that follow provide examples and case studies of these behaviors. As you read through them, you might want to mark those you believe apply to you.

You might be wondering how, if experience shapes behavior, you are supposed to let go of habits and responses that have become ingrained over years or even decades in the workplace.

Isn't there truth in the familiar adage that "you can't teach an old dog new tricks"?

The good news is that we now know the old-dog adage doesn't apply to humans. It doesn't even apply to dogs! Until recently, brain researchers believed that only children's neural systems had the capacity to change by growing the new circuits that new skills and new behaviors require. But functional MRIs (fMRIs), which allow neuroscientists to view the brain in operation, instead confirm that the brain retains the capacity to build fresh neural pathways at every stage of healthy adulthood.

As a result, you *can* rewire your brain to support new habits and thought patterns at any time during your life. The only catch is that you must be willing to repeat these new behaviors until your brain gets comfortable with them. That's because behaviors and thoughts build new pathways *only when repeated over time*. With practice, they become established and begin to operate by default. Even people who have suffered profound trauma can heal by repeating habits and thoughts that counteract established responses.

This principle of neuroplasticity means that you have the ability to change how you respond to situations. Past experiences may shape your behavior, but they need not *determine* it. You have the power to become more precise, more intentional, more present, more assertive, more autonomous, more at ease exercising authority, more confident setting boundaries, and a more effective advocate for yourself.

All these riches lie within your capacity and scope. But the process can't start until you identify those habits that hold you back, and start practicing new habits that better serve you.

With this positive news in mind, we present the twelve behaviors that we most often observe keeping women stuck.

1. Reluctance to claim your achievements
2. Expecting others to spontaneously notice and reward your contributions
3. Overvaluing expertise
4. Just building rather than building and leveraging relationships
5. Failing to enlist allies from day one
6. Putting your job before your career
7. The perfection trap
8. The disease to please
9. Minimizing
10. Too much
11. Ruminating
12. Letting your radar distract you

LIMITING BEHAVIORS ARE ALSO STRENGTHS

As Marshall points out in *What Got You Here*, the higher you go in your organization, the more likely your problems are to be behavioral. You don't lack skills. You are clearly smart. You're good at coping and at thinking strategically. You've got experience, and the gravitas that comes with it. You've probably built a lot of useful connections over the years. You're clear about your values and ethics. You're accustomed to following through. You're probably an excellent communicator. You are highly disciplined, and you are motivated.

Success usually indicates that you've got the basics of your job down. Which is why behavioral issues become so important. If you still perceive barriers that keep you from getting where you want to go, behavioral impediments are likely to play a key role. Of course, as a woman you may still encounter cultural and structural barriers in your organization. There's no point in denying that these still exist. But as noted earlier, culture and structure don't lie within your control, whereas your behaviors and habits do. So that's always the best place to start improving the quality of your life at work and your prospects for reaching your full potential.

One caveat.

As you drill down on the habits described in the next chapters, you may get nudges of recognition and find yourself thinking, *Wow, does this ever sound like me!* This is a good thing, since being open to information about limiting behaviors is the essential first step on the path toward making healthy and long-lasting change.

But try to avoid being too hard on yourself or identifying too many items you need to get to work on, as even Frances Hesselbein did in Chapter 1. If you do, you may start feeling overwhelmed.

Marshall's experience conducting 360-degree feedback consistently shows that women in organizations are perceived as being more effective leaders than men. Many people find this surprising—not that women are more effective leaders, but that it's the widely held perception about specific women inside an organization. This doesn't mean that *every* woman is seen as more effective. It means that the average woman is statistically viewed as a better leader than the average man. It's a reassuring and empowering message for women to understand.

But Marshall's feedback analysis also makes clear that women are much harder on themselves than men are. They tend to worry more about their perceived faults and feel greater pressure to make improvements. This can be useful because it makes you willing to change. But getting caught up in self-reproach, or beating yourself up for being a flawed human being, is always counterproductive. You can't lead, and you can't make helpful improvements in your behavior, if you're constantly berating yourself.

That's why Marshall's ground-rule request when coaching women is, "Please do not be too hard on yourself."

We urge you to keep this in mind. We also urge you to recognize what got you to wherever you are today. The flip side of every limiting behavior is always a strength. Strengths such as empathy, humility, diligence, and reliability underlie many of the behaviors described in this book. So as you read through these behaviors and think about what you would like to work on, please take time to recognize and celebrate what got you here.

Now let's figure out what it's going to take for you to rise to the next level.

CHAPTER 5

Habit 1: Reluctance to Claim Your Achievements

Over the years, Sally has conducted in-depth interviews with countless women leaders. Several years ago, she spent days interviewing senior female partners in accounting, law, consulting, and investment firms. She was interested in learning what they believed had been most responsible for their success, and particularly eager to get their thoughts about how younger women in their firms might better position themselves to become partners.

The responses to her questions ran a wide gamut, but in two areas were remarkably consistent. When asked about the greatest strength of the younger women in their firms, the female partners almost unanimously cited their ability to deliver high-quality work. "The women here go the extra mile when you give them assignments," said one partner. Said another, "They are extremely conscientious, crossing every *t* and dotting every *i*. They take deadlines seriously. They show up. They are meticulous. You can count on them to get the job done."

When asked what the younger women in their firms were *worst* at, the responses were also consistent. "Hands down, they are worst at bringing attention and visibility to their successes." "They often work harder than their male peers but then go out of their way to avoid taking credit for what they've done, especially with senior leaders." "A lot of our women seem uncomfortable using the 'I' word, so they always try to spread the credit around. This might make them good people but it doesn't help their careers."

These observations were all made about associates in partnership firms, such as law, accounting, consulting, and investment banking. But reluctance to claim achievements is common among women in every sector and at every level. When delivering workshops to high-potential younger workers and women leaders, Sally often makes reference to her partnership survey and asks, "How many of you are good at drawing attention to what you achieve?" Usually, only scattered hands go up. Sometimes, not a single woman describes herself this way.

When asked to reflect on *why* they struggle with claiming their achievements, answers vary. But two responses surface nearly every time:

"If I have to act like that obnoxious blowhard down the hall to get noticed around here, I'd prefer to be ignored. I have no desire to behave like that jerk."

And:

"I believe great work speaks for itself. If I do an outstanding job, people *should* notice."

We will examine this second response in the next chapter, when we look at Habit 2. But for now, let's unpack the "obnoxious blowhard" answer. It's quite common. A woman will pick out the most shameless self-promoter in the organization and decide that, if she tries to draw attention to what she's doing, she will be acting like him. (It's usually a him.) Since the thought of emulating this insufferable colleague's behavior repels her, she prefers to keep her head down instead of looking for ways to get recognized for her contributions.

There are two problems with this approach.

First, citing the jerk down the hall as an example of everything you are not and don't wish to become indicates an either/or way of thinking. *Either* you exemplify the worst aspects of a given behavior, *or* you behave in an entirely opposite manner. Either/or thinking sees no possibility of a middle ground, no graceful way, for example, to bring attention to the quality of your work without becoming obnoxious and self-serving, and so justifies your refusal to do so. Either/or is a common trap, something you'll be hearing a lot about in this book, and a pitfall you will benefit from avoiding.

Second, contrasting your refusal to claim credit for your own good work with an extreme opposite example can inspire you to feel morally superior to anyone who is comfortable doing so. This is unhelpful, because it gives you an excuse for buying into what is ultimately a rationale for staying in your comfort zone. Instead of asking yourself *why* you have trouble bringing attention to your successes and then figuring out an appropriate way to do so, you congratulate yourself for being a wonderful human being who doesn't need to toot her own horn. And then you try to take solace in that when you're passed over for the next promotion.

Marshall notes that people generally tailor their behavior to meet the expectations of their "referent group." It's a phrase he picked up from the late great diversity pioneer Roosevelt Thomas. Basically it means that people act the way the group they identify with expects them to act. If you feel uncomfortable drawing attention to your achievements, it's often because your referent group—other women, a former boss, a repressive culture, your family of origin—expects you to be modest and self-effacing.

As a result, you tend to view behaviors that don't meet these expectations as disruptive. And you avoid them even in professional situations where they are expected. But think about it. If women in the seventies, eighties, and nineties had been universally concerned with meeting the expectations of their referent group, there would be about zero women in management ranks today. Moving ahead—rising—requires bold action. So while there's nothing to gain from being obnoxious, shrinking into yourself in an effort to please isn't going to benefit you—or other women.

INVISIBLE IN PITTSBURGH

Consider Amy, the executive director of a small but highly regarded arts foundation in Pittsburgh. Filling out a questionnaire in one of Sally's workshops, she ranked herself a 5, the lowest possible grade on a scale of 1–5, on her ability to gain recognition for her work, and a corresponding 1 (the top grade) on her ability to deliver outstanding results.

Until recently, Amy hadn't considered this gap to be a problem. She was the oldest in a large Catholic family and had been raised to put the needs of others first. She considered her willingness to do so a virtue. But she'd recently had a wake-up call that caused her to question her reluctance to claim her own achievements.

She had co-chaired a high-profile charity event that attracted top corporate leaders in the city and raised more than double the money its sponsors had expected. She shared the considerable work the benefit entailed with a male co-chair—let's call him Mitch—who headed the largest social service nonprofit in western Pennsylvania. Amy and Mitch worked well together and delivered outstanding results. She believed they'd developed a strong working relationship.

On the day following the event, a local reporter called to interview Amy. He asked what she believed had contributed to the event's remarkable success. She spoke effusively about her collaboration with Mitch and lauded his efforts, citing specific actions as well as donors he had brought on board. She also credited everyone on their team for their hard work, superb planning, and ability to bring top players in the community together.

When the article appeared the next day, it nearly sent Amy into shock. The reporter who interviewed her had also spoken with Mitch, but how Mitch chose to describe the event stood in stark contrast to Amy's description. "I couldn't believe it," she said. "He never even mentioned me. He basically took credit for everything that had gone right and used the interview to promote himself and his organization. Since I also spent most of my time giving him credit, he came off as the linchpin and sole driving force behind the event. People all over town were calling to congratulate him. I thought we'd been a real team, but apparently he didn't see it that way. I had no idea he was so self-centered."

A sympathetic murmur went through the workshop as Amy told her story. Yet it's helpful to step back and consider what might really be going on. Mitch is the regional director of an international nonprofit, and a big part of his job is making his regional organization look good. He is also, not surprisingly, interested in sending his prestigious board the message that he is doing a stellar job. Maybe he's eager to stay in the job and knows a younger candidate is nipping at his heels. Or perhaps he's thinking about his upcoming contract negotiation and wants to be sure his board recognizes his value.

Do taking these considerations into account really make Mitch self-centered? He may or may not be, but using the newspaper interview to promote his role and his organization doesn't provide proof either way.

The more relevant question is why Amy, given the chance to shine a light on her work, felt compelled to spend the entire interview talking up Mitch. Clearly, he's a successful leader who has no problem speaking for himself. Why did she feel the need to speak for him?

Talking at greater length not only with Amy but also later with Mitch gave Sally some insight into how things had gone wrong. To begin with, Amy noted that she was trying to demonstrate the kind of collegiality she associates with superb nonprofit leaders. But she also said she felt comfortable putting the spotlight on Mitch because she assumed he would do the same for her when being interviewed by the reporter. "I figured he'd be talking about me and my contributions to the event, just as I'd highlighted what he brought to the table."

Mitch, by contrast, said it never occurred to him that Amy would fail to speak on her own behalf. "After all," he said, "the reporter was giving her an opportunity to position herself and her organization very nicely and raise both their profiles in the community and beyond. I'm not sure why she didn't see it that way, but it's not my job to carry her water. She's in a leadership position, doesn't she know how this works?"

Clearly, Amy and Mitch were operating from entirely different premises. She used the interview as an opportunity to be generous and supportive, while he focused on doing what he perceived to be his job.

For a while, Amy comforted herself with the notion that she'd shown herself to be a better person than Mitch. But she received a rude jolt when she learned that her board was less than thrilled with her failure to give adequate attention to the foundation on whose behalf they were working. Painful as this was, hearing of the board's displeasure from its chair finally spurred Amy to action. Instead of dismissing Mitch as a showboat, she decided to figure out how to become a more effective advocate for herself and her organization.

That's when Amy realized she was in the *habit* of turning the spotlight onto other people. If a colleague commented on her well-run office, she automatically credited her assistant. If a donor told her he'd received a strong report on a partnership initiative she had led, she praised the partner. This kind of behavior felt normal to her, a gracious way of responding and very much in line with how she'd been raised.

But given the pushback she'd received from her board, she began to wonder if something else might also be at work. Was she simply uncomfortable accepting praise or claiming credit? Was she overly invested in her modest self-image? She recalled a friend once pointing out that whenever Amy was given a compliment, she used it as an opportunity to point out her own flaws. "Why contradict someone who says something nice?" her friend had asked.

Amy consulted a coach, who suggested she start addressing her unwillingness to accept credit by simply saying *thank you* whenever she was praised. The coach had trained with Marshall, and one of the chief behaviors Marshall works to instill in his clients is the habit of saying thank you—and then nothing more. No "thank you... *but my whole team worked so hard it was easy.*" No "thank you... *we got lucky with the weather, didn't we?*" No deferrals, no false modesty, no protestations. Simply *thank you.* Marshall has gone so far as to impose fines on clients who fail to follow this rule.

At first, Amy found herself responding with some version of, "thank you, but it really wasn't difficult." In other words, she accepted credit while also deflecting it. But she kept trying and was soon able to drop the elaboration. She says, "It sounds simple, but I realized that forcing myself to stop at *thank you* was a good way to start practicing a new behavior. If I could get in the habit of accepting credit, maybe I could get more comfortable claiming it. That will help me and my organization."

THE I IN TEAM

Amy had enjoyed a successful career in nonprofits despite her self-effacing modesty. But her long-indulged allergy to self-promotion got her into trouble when she reached the top position. This is common. As you move to a higher level, any discomfort you feel claiming recognition will begin to incur higher costs. That's because when you represent your organization as Amy does, diverting credit not only diminishes your own achievements, it undercuts the visibility of the people you work with: colleagues, employees, partners, senior leaders, and, in Amy's case, her board.

Organizations often fail to address women's reluctance to effectively market themselves because they assume a male leadership template. Sally got a sense of how ingrained this assumption can be a few years ago when participating in a women's leadership forum at one of the big four accounting firms. The regional event was held at a resort outside Atlanta.

Since she was moderating two panels, Sally had interviewed a number of senior women at the firm in advance and delivered the quick quiz she'd used in the workshop with Amy to every participant. The results made clear that, although many of the women were confident of their ability to deliver outstanding results, they struggled with getting recognized for their work. Many shared the kind of self-effacing habits that had been a problem for Amy, rating themselves at the low end of the scale when it came to recognition.

Nevertheless, the HR team that organized the event chose to send a very different message about the goals of the company and the habits and behaviors they wanted to reinforce. It turns out that a recent firm-wide assessment showed that 40 percent of the organization's senior leaders were viewed as "reluctant to share information or credit." (The fact that those senior leaders were mostly men may have influenced those results!) As a consequence, the powers that be decided to focus every leadership event in the coming year on instilling a spirit of teamwork among employees. The HR team planning the women's forum therefore chose "There Is No I in Team" as its theme. Colorful banners proclaimed the slogan at the entrance to the venue and above the stage where the panelists sat. Sam, a top executive, urged participants in his opening keynote to make an effort to share credit for achievements.

To Sally, the scene provided a perfect example of why companies often get women's leadership wrong and misunderstand the nature of women's challenges. For many of the attendees, putting an *I* in team was hardly the problem. Instead they struggled to use the word *I* in talking about their successes. As one participant said at the cocktail party following the panel, "I appreciated what Sam had to say, but I didn't identify with it. In my experience, our women have more problems with self-marketing than with bragging. I know I do."

THE ART OF SELF-PROMOTION

If you struggle to claim credit for your achievements, it may cost you throughout your career. But the costs will be highest when you're trying to move to the next level or seeking a new job. Speaking up about what you contribute and detailing why you're qualified does not make you self-centered or self-serving. It sends a signal that you're ready to rise.

Search firms confirm that women applying for jobs are often less assertive than men when it comes to declaring their qualifications. Fern, a partner in a firm that places health care professionals, says, "We find women are often tentative when describing their skills and experience. It's not uncommon to come across comments in application letters such as, 'I've never held a position like this before so I'm not sure if my qualifications are an exact match.'"

A less qualified man will often be bolder, Fern reports. "A guy might say, 'I have exactly the skills you are looking for and can easily meet these requirements because I'm excellent at X, Y, and Z.' Maybe X, Y, and Z have nothing to do with the job, but his confidence somehow manages to convince you. Whereas women are more likely to express doubt. All too often, this results in the job going to the less qualified man. Since he so firmly believes he can do the job, the employer is willing to give him a chance. Of course, sometimes sexism is at work, but often the woman is just too hesitant in making the case that she's ready. When that happens, it's very discouraging."

Effectively marketing yourself, far from being shameful, is an important part of every job—and key to helping you reach the next level of success. If you want to reach your highest potential, making your achievements visible, especially to those at senior levels, is as important as the actual tasks spelled out in your job description.

If you don't find a way to speak about the value of what you're doing, you send a message that you don't put much value on it. And if *you* don't value it, why should anyone else? You also communicate that you may be ambivalent about getting ahead. And if *you're* ambivalent, why should anyone stick his neck out to support you?

If you're considering how you might promote yourself, it helps to bear in mind that you are your primary product. As you talk about what you have achieved, you are always selling you—not just the details but the overall package. Every successful salesperson knows this. People buy because they like and trust you. And because they believe what you offer may have value for them. Why do they believe this? Because you so obviously do! Mesmerizing belief is the secret of every great salesperson.

To sell yourself effectively, therefore, believing in what you have to offer is essential. If Coke is doing a marketing campaign, they don't say, "*Well, some people prefer Pepsi. Or, it's possible that, if you give Coke a try, you might like it.*" No. Their job is to talk about how great Coke is. Not to hedge, but to come out and tell the world, "We've got a fantastic product."

If this sort of declaration makes you uncomfortable, it may help to think in terms of *why* it matters that you get ahead. What ultimately motivates you in your quest? If simply reaching the top of the hierarchical peak isn't enough, maybe something else gets your juices flowing.

Maybe you believe that your having more power in the organization would be great for your wonderful clients. Maybe you think that your organization could benefit from having someone with your emotional IQ at the top. Maybe you're convinced that you would be a good leader—or at least better than the bullying colleague who's angling for the job you want. Maybe you think your company would benefit if more women held high positions. Maybe you want to inspire your kids or give your parents something to feel great about.

Please note: these are not self-serving reasons. But they may be reasons that motivate you. If so, keep them in mind the next time you feel tempted to deflect credit for your achievements, or say "it was nothing" or "anybody could have done what I did." The world can benefit from your success.

What else can help? Exposing the fallacy of either/or thinking could be a start. So you think you are either a shameless self-promoter *or* a self-effacing martyr beavering away at her job? No, there's a lot of ground in between these polar opposites. You can simply be a talented person bent on speaking up for herself. Look for the nuance in situations, and find a middle ground between "shrinking violet" and "shrill self-publicist" that feels right to you.

And if you still think of effectively marketing yourself as cheesy or beneath you, you might try looking at it through an upside-down lens. For example, Marshall has observed that men sometimes mistrust women who are averse to claiming their achievements. They view such women as inauthentic, falsely humble, or lacking in commitment. So why would you let your behavior support such negative perceptions?

If claiming your achievements feels like a new behavior for you, you might want to try enlisting a colleague to help you. You'll find lots of ideas for how to do this in Chapter 18 of this book. For example, you might start by simply asking a peer who worked with you on a successful venture to speak a bit on your behalf the next time you're in a meeting. It might not be boldly taking the initiative yourself, but it will be a step.

Just refrain from contradicting what they have to say.

CHAPTER 6

Habit 2: Expecting Others to Spontaneously Notice and Reward Your Contributions

In the last chapter, we examined how failing to claim your achievements can impede your rise in your company or your career. The flip side of this habit is expecting others to notice your contributions without your having to draw attention to them yourself. These two behaviors work together. They have similar roots but different effects. Together, they can really keep you stuck.

As noted earlier, the women in Sally's workshops who say they're no good at drawing attention to their achievements usually give one of two reasons. There's the obnoxious blowhard answer, which we examined in the previous chapter. And then there's the that's-not-my-job answer, most often expressed as the belief that "great work should speak for itself." Or, "If I do an outstanding job, people *should* notice."

These beliefs can serve as a convenient excuse for refusing to claim your achievements, letting you off the hook (in your own mind at least) if advocating for yourself makes you feel awkward. You might believe your reluctance is appropriate, or evidence that you're a superior sort of person, but it can sabotage your best efforts and result in your hard work being overlooked.

This is what happened to Amy, the nonprofit head described in the previous chapter who assumed her co-chair Mitch would talk up her contributions when the newspaper reporter interviewed him. It's what happened to Ellen, the Silicon Valley engineer introduced in Chapter 1, who felt devastated when her boss failed to notice the connections she had built in the company, even though he had no actual way of knowing how many people she routinely reached out to.

Expecting others to notice your contributions, or believing that they should, is not only a good way to keep yourself stuck, it can also diminish the satisfaction you feel in a job you would otherwise enjoy. Remember this: Companies don't just make great products and assume that customers "should" want to buy them. They have a marketing function that is designed to effectively promote what they do. You, as a professional, need one too. Otherwise, when the praise you hope for is not forthcoming, you might feel unappreciated and under-acknowledged. You may start to resent not only the higher-ups who seem unaware of all the hard work you do but also colleagues who are skilled at getting noticed. You may then decide they're just showboats and congratulate yourself on being less self-centered, taking comfort in your own wonderfulness even as you stay in the shadows.

If you get entrenched in this kind of negative thinking, you may start believing you don't really belong in your job. After all, if the people around you are incapable of noticing your efforts, maybe you'd be better off somewhere else. This is how a job that seems like a perfect fit when you sign on to it starts to lose its attraction. Which is just another reason why taking a more proactive approach than expecting to be noticed is so important.

MAUREEN'S BIG LESSON

Maureen is a senior partner in a premier San Francisco law firm. Despite her stellar early performance, she made partner later than a number of the men who joined the firm the same year she did. This made her feel so undervalued that, at the start of her fifth year as an associate, she decided the firm wasn't a good fit for her.

When a client approached her about a position in his company's general counsel's office, she met with him several times. Then, with great trepidation, she let her practice head know she was looking around.

"Would you consider staying if you were made partner?" he asked.

Without hesitating, Maureen said yes.

"Assume it's going to happen," he told her. "Don't make any move till it does. I don't think the members of our partnership committee realized you were set on it."

How could they not have? Maureen asked herself, though she did not put the question to her practice head. Hadn't anyone in the firm noticed that she'd been working her tail off since the day she arrived? Given her record of achievement, why on earth would they *not* have assumed partnership was her goal? Did they imagine she wanted to be an associate for the rest of her life?

Two months after the conversation with her practice head, Maureen was made partner. She stayed on and has now been with the firm for fourteen years. Three years ago, she was invited to join the firm's prestigious partnership committee, which evaluates candidates and chooses partners. Seeing how this process actually works and how other members of the committee think, she finally understood why it had taken her so long to be promoted.

She says, "At my first meeting, we gathered around a conference table to consider two successful associates, a woman and a man. Both had entered the firm the same year and both had made their mark in corporate litigation. The head of our litigation practice had glowing things to say about both of them. But in the course of our discussion, he mentioned that the man seemed to want it more. He warned that the firm would lose him if he weren't promoted that year."

Maureen knew the female associate and had a high opinion of her. She was particularly skilled at client management, which was crucial at the time because one of the firm's long-standing corporate clients was reevaluating how it allocated litigation work. "I brought this up and said I thought her skills were particularly needed given the challenge we were facing. I said I hadn't seen the male associate exhibit the same level of attention to client work."

The litigation head agreed with Maureen's assessment, but said he was reluctant to lose the male associate to a competing firm. Maureen asked why he believed the associate would leave if he weren't promoted in this round.

"That's easy," he said. "The guy has been talking about making partner since his first day here. He's totally motivated by the desire and expects it to happen in his first year of eligibility. If we don't give it to him now, I guarantee we'll lose him to the first firm that makes an offer."

"What about Jill?" Maureen asked. "Won't she expect to be made partner as well?"

"Maybe," he responded. "But she's never said anything about it or pushed to be considered. She seems to enjoy the work for its own sake. I know she likes our practice group and has strong ties to her clients. So I wouldn't expect her to leave if she weren't chosen this year."

There it is, thought Maureen. *That's the reason it took me so long to make partner. I didn't start talking about it the moment I arrived. It never occurred to me to do that. I figured if I did outstanding work, I would be chosen when the time came. I assumed that was how things worked.*

The next three years on the committee taught Maureen that this situation was not unique—not for her and not for Jill, the associate whose name came up at that first meeting. "Time and again, I heard the same rationale for promoting a man earlier than a woman: *he wants it more, he's been lobbying for it since he arrived, he'll never stay if he's not chosen.* My big takeaway was that the associates who constantly talk about being made partner get identified as partner material because they're so obviously hungry and ambitious. The ones who don't—unfortunately, it's usually the women—get overlooked."

Maureen's experience led her to conclude that the common female strategy of working as hard as possible and trusting that would get you noticed was a key reason the women in her firm made partner later in their careers than men. And these delays had consequences. When women saw men being promoted earlier year after year, they concluded that the firm didn't value them or recognize their potential. And so they began to look around, as Maureen had. The resulting attrition confirmed the belief among senior partners that women were more likely to leave than men, so they tended to view the women as less committed.

Maureen says, "It amazed me to realize that the women's tendency to focus on their work rather than effectively communicating what they were doing got interpreted as a lack of commitment. This seemed counterintuitive, because you'd think hard work would demonstrate loyalty. Certainly that's what I'd always assumed. But when the senior partners heard someone constantly announcing his desire to become partner, they saw it as evidence that he wanted to build a career at the firm." Since women were less likely to talk about it, the firm leaders tended to question whether they were in it for the long term.

Not surprisingly, the motherhood issue often came into play here. Says Maureen, "When a woman's name came up for consideration, you'd hear things like, 'She's probably not that interested in making partner now because she's at the age for having children.' I'd point out that most of our female partners had children, and that they shouldn't assume a woman wasn't interested in making partner because she was a certain age. It took a while, but the committee finally figured out a simple solution. Which was to ask the woman how *she* saw her future in the firm."

This shift set in motion a chain of events that expanded the pool of women being considered for partner, which in turn began to slow female attrition. The bottom line, says Maureen, is that "there will always be guys at our firm who start saying 'I'm totally awesome' on the day they arrive. Because they say it, partners used to assume it was true. Now they're getting used to the idea that there isn't a direct corollary between who is 'partner material' and who just *says* they are. But it took some work to get here."

As a result of her experience, Maureen became passionate about letting women entering the firm know how important it is to take responsibility for getting noticed. "I tell them, say what you're doing, say what you've accomplished, and say what motivates you. If you want to make partner, you need to say so, over and over. If you don't, the top dogs won't view you as committed. Just working hard won't get you where you want to go."

ON THE ELEVATOR

So how do you start taking responsibility for assuring your work gets noticed? How do you draw attention to what you contribute without feeling like a self-centered jerk? You might start by articulating a vision of where you would like your job to take you so you can give people a context for what you want in your future. Then prepare yourself to take advantage of any opportunities to share what you see.

This is an approach advocated by Dong Lao, who serves as executive sponsor for the women's initiative at a London-based global financial institution. In addition to being a world-class banker, Lao works with the women in his organization to identify how to secure the resources they need to get ahead. During a recent conference at an off-site in Switzerland, a participant asked him during the large plenary session what *one thing* he thought women could do to better position themselves for leadership in the organization.

He responded with a story about finding himself in the elevator at the bank's London headquarters a few months before. A young male analyst who had recently joined the organization was standing next to him when a high-profile senior official stepped inside. Says Lao, "The young man was from the Middle East. Very polished, obviously confident, but also polite. Not swaggering or arrogant like some of our headquarters hires.

"The official had no idea who the analyst was since people at headquarters don't connect much across levels. But as the elevator started to move, the executive asked the young man what he did at the bank. Without a moment's hesitation, he responded with three clear and succinct sentences. He mentioned his present job, said his goal was to lead a telecom investment team in south Asia, and noted ties between his country of origin and the region he hoped to work in as well as two key relationships that would be useful. The little speech took less than a minute but was packed with information. He'd clearly given thought to every word and thoroughly rehearsed it."

When the spiel was finished, the analyst stopped speaking and handed his card to the official, who then held the elevator door open as he got off. "I'm going to pass this along to the head of our subcontinent investment team," he said. "If you don't hear from him, let his office know I personally told you to call."

"Why am I telling you this story?" Lao asked his audience. "Because I believe many of you can learn from it. Having a clear, concise statement ready to deliver at any moment—one that says what you do now but emphasizes what you want to do in the future and why you're qualified to do it—gives you a huge advantage in terms of visibility and positioning. It sets you apart from the pack and enables you to make the case for yourself at the highest level when the chance presents itself. In my experience, great careers are often built on chance encounters. So it always pays to be prepared."

Lao noted three advantages to having an elevator speech memorized and ready to go. "First, it shows you're ambitious, and that your ambition is focused on something specific that you're working to achieve. Second, it gives you an opportunity to talk about your skills or background in a way that aligns with what could be useful to the organization, not just now but in the years ahead. You're not blowing hot air, you're telling a story about why you have what it takes to move up and, by implication, how the organization can benefit from that. Third, it gives you a chance to show that you're thoughtful, reflective, and concise—the last being important to executives who are always pressed for time and in the habit of asking people to bottom-line it."

What was particularly impressive, said Lao, was how the young man stopped speaking once he had said his piece. "He didn't ramble on or try to fill the time. He came to a full stop and handed over his card. Mission accomplished."

Lao suggested each participant at the conference work on developing an elevator speech, a clear and concise summary of what she does, what she wants to do in the future, and why she believes she's the right person to do it. He said, "The most important things are that it's real, a true statement of what you could see yourself doing in the future and have a desire to do. And that it's as brief as you can possibly make it. No background, no extra details, no explanations, justifications, ifs, or hedges. You want to keep it as short and clear and strong as you can."

Lao also advised not worrying that what you have to say might change over time. "If that happens, you'll develop a new elevator speech. The goal is to be prepared to stake a claim for yourself and your future so that when the chance to connect with a senior leader falls in your lap, you can seize it. You want to get noticed, and create opportunities for yourself. If they change over time, that's all to the good."

HAVING A YARDSTICK

The elevator speech Lao describes is a tactical version of a vision or mission statement, a personal articulation of purpose that declares what you're trying to achieve in the world. Peter Drucker, a major influence on both of us and someone we both knew personally, and with whom Marshall worked, was the first to speak about the importance of having such a statement, both for organizations and for individuals.

Peter Drucker once told Marshall, "You should be able to put your mission statement on a T-shirt." Marshall believes this small bit of advice changed his life. Developed years ago, Marshall's mission is clear and simple, to become the world authority on "Helping successful leaders achieve positive, lasting change in behavior." It worked! Today, if you do a Google search for "helping successful leaders" (in quotes), of the first 500 results, approximately 450 are about Marshall.

A crystal clear sense of what you're trying to do and why you are motivated to do it not only enables you to speak your truth powerfully and concisely, it also helps you clarify which opportunities you want to embrace and which you should let go of. You simply ask yourself, *Would doing this help me reach my larger goal?* If so, you might want to say yes. If not, you have a solid reason for saying no.

Miranda in Chapter 2 could have used such a yardstick when a colleague tried to enlist her to do some drudge work on her law firm's recruitment committee. If she'd had a clearer, more articulated sense of what she wanted to achieve, she could have used it to evaluate whether the opportunity served her or not. This would have helped her know what questions to ask her colleague. And it would have made it easier to turn down the request if it didn't fit with her plans for her future.

Creating an elevator speech can pay many dividends. It can help you think more clearly about your future. It can make you feel more confident and prepared. It can mark you as serious, a potential player, someone to watch. And it's perfect for moving beyond the passive trap of hoping to be noticed.

CHAPTER 7

Habit 3: Overvaluing Expertise

Trying to master every detail of your job in order to become an expert is a great strategy for keeping the job you have. But if your goal is to move to a higher level, your expertise is probably not going to get you there. In fact, mastery of your current role often serves as a useful strategy for keeping yourself in your current role.

If you find this statement shocking, it may be because, like many women, you've assumed expertise is the surest route to success. And so you put enormous effort into learning every aspect of your job and assuring your work is letter-perfect. This feels proactive, but it can set you up to remain on an endless treadmill, constantly setting a higher bar for yourself as you seek to always go the extra mile. Meanwhile, your male colleagues are taking a different route, trying to do the job well enough while focusing their time on building the relationships and visibility that will get them to the next level.

Of course, we're not advocating sloppy performance. And we know that skill and knowledge are required for success. But if you want to rise in your field or your organization, expertise will only take you so far. That's because the top jobs always require managing and leading people who have expertise, not providing expertise yourself.

It's only natural that women would want to become experts at what they do, since it's how women earned their spot at the table in the first place. Especially if you're in a career, sector, or company with relatively few women, you may have had to prove your competence from the day you arrived. Maybe your first boss doubted your ability, and you had to make an extra effort to convince him you could handle the job. Maybe a male colleague resented your being on his team, so you tried to earn his respect by becoming a supercontributor—making his job easier in the process. Or maybe you lacked confidence or feared you didn't really belong, and so worked extra hard to prove to yourself that you deserved a seat at the table. Whatever the reason, your experiences are bound to have shaped your behavior, and over time your behavior may have become habitual. Your commitment to expertise may have helped you survive and may have gotten you where you are today. But as you move higher, it may start to get in your way.

In *Necessary Dreams*, Anna Fels notes that feeling fulfilled at work requires two things: mastery and recognition. Mastery is the expertise part, the sheer enjoyment you feel when you do something you value really well. Mastery provides what psychologists call an intrinsic reward, meaning you take satisfaction from it. The effort and the reward are both internal.

Fels's second requirement for workplace fulfillment is being recognized for what you do. Recognition is an extrinsic reward because it comes from the outside: you need someone else to recognize you. It's not surprising, then, that women tend to overvalue expertise, since women often have a tougher time being recognized for their achievements.

As noted in the previous chapter, women are often under-recognized because they're uncomfortable claiming their achievements. If talking yourself up or drawing attention to what you've accomplished makes you feel like a self-important jerk, you probably prefer to keep your head down and hope that others notice what you're contributing. But women are also at times under-recognized because the people around them undervalue their contributions. This is not uncommon, particularly in sectors like science and medicine, where undervaluing female achievement is well documented and has a long tradition.

When you're routinely under-recognized, expertise can become a defense, your way of asserting your value regardless of what others perceive or think. Being intrinsic, mastery is the one source of satisfaction that you can control. This is a good thing, and can be deeply rewarding. But it's insufficient if you want to move ahead.

THE MASTERY MIND-SET

A great example is Ashley, one of the featured speakers at a Denver gathering Sally attended of Colorado's top women leaders. At the age of thirty, Ashley had recently been promoted to head her company's huge business-to-business services group. When asked what was most responsible for her meteoric rise, she surprised her audience by saying, "It was learning to let go of being an expert."

Ashley explained: "My biggest career lesson has been learning that, while expertise is *expected* in almost any job, it doesn't do much to help you get ahead. It took me a while to see this. When I joined the company, there were very few women, and I worried about being up to the job. I certainly lacked the confidence of the guys around me. They got a lot of confirmation and seemed comfortable with all the politics. I felt I had to watch my step and earn my way, so I focused on learning every detail, becoming expert in every task, proving my value, and avoiding criticism. Which is fine, but it's a poor way to position yourself for something bigger."

This is true for several reasons. First, learning every detail to perfection uses up a lot of bandwidth, leaving you little time to develop the relationships you need to move ahead. Second, your efforts to do everything perfectly usually have the effect of demonstrating that you're perfect for the job you already have. Third, the expertise you develop may make you indispensable to your boss, who will quite logically want to keep you where you are.

This last scenario provided Ashley with her wake-up call. She'd been with the company six years when her boss mentioned that her name had surfaced for a job in the company's fast-growing business-to-business division. "He told me the internal recruiter was interested, but that he, my boss, couldn't afford to lose me," Ashley says. "It's amazing he didn't think telling me this would be a problem. But even more amazing is that I saw nothing wrong with it. I actually felt flattered that he needed me so much. It was the validation I'd been looking for since joining the company"— that extrinsic endorsement that means so much to all of us.

Yet her boss's mention of B2B stayed with her, and after watching two less qualified colleagues get juicy promotions, Ashley realized her "mastery mind-set" approach to her current role was virtually designed to keep her stuck. She sought counsel from a former boss, who told her she needed to think of every job as both a job *and* a bridge to whatever comes next.

He said, "Of course you need to deliver on your work, but you've got to think bigger than that. It's rare to get promoted because you've done your job flawlessly. You're most likely to get promoted because people know you and trust that you could be contributing at a higher level. And because you demonstrate you're ready for a challenge."

That conversation turned Ashley around. "I realized I had basically told my present boss I was content to remain where I was. Now I had to show him this was no longer true. So when an even bigger job in B2B was posted, I marched into his office and told him I would slit my wrists to get it. He couldn't have been more surprised, but he heard me. I'd certainly made myself clear! He said he'd be glad to give me his support."

Ashley followed up with an e-mail to her boss that laid out all the reasons she was right for the new position. "Basically, they were talking points he could use to sell me to the B2B team. He told me having it all written out really helped him."

It also helped Ashley because composing the e-mail required her to think deep and hard about her strengths. This changed her picture of what she had to contribute. She says, "I'd always taken for granted that being diligent and super-conscientious was what made me successful in the jobs I'd held. But looking beneath the surface, I saw that my skill at managing relationships was actually my biggest asset. That's what really qualified me for the next job. This was a big aha for me. It gave me confidence and a way to tell my new boss I was ready for even bigger things. More important, it helped *me* see that I was ready."

UP FROM THE BENCH

Ana, a software designer with one of the biggest tech firms in Silicon Valley, learned a similar lesson about the limited value of pure expertise. But she learned it on her own, without the intervention of a former boss.

Ana grew up in Mexico but went to engineering school in California, where she was one of very few women. One of her professors made clear that, in his view, teaching female engineers was a waste of time.

Says Ana, "He used to say right in class that of course all the women would get jobs because companies were being forced to hire us. He saw it as affirmative action and didn't expect any of us to do well. When he said that, he used to look straight at me. I got the idea he saw me as a double affirmative action case because I stood out as a Latina."

Ana did manage to land a job developing software in a company that was actively recruiting women, so her professor's comments continued to ring in her head. She wanted to prove she'd been hired based on her merit, so she focused on outperforming on her assignments and being the most reliable workhorse on her team.

She says, "I didn't think about moving higher. I was grateful to have a good job and enjoyed being methodical and competent while building my skills as an engineer. I probably would have been content to stay where I was, but my husband died suddenly, leaving me with three young children to support. I knew I would need full-time childcare and have to provide for my kids in a very expensive part of the world. That meant I needed to move up."

Ana began applying for high-potential positions and soon got fast-tracked into a job developing new systems for the legal profession. She says, "It was a totally different environment. Instead of engineers working at their benches, we were constantly connecting with our clients so we could figure out what *they* needed. I knew nothing about law firms so I started setting up a lot of meetings where I could talk to lawyers about how they used technology."

Ana's job in those meetings was to ask questions, listen, and learn. At first, this made her uncomfortable. "I felt I should be conveying information or somehow showing I knew enough to be there. When I'd done presentations in my old job, there was always a huge amount of prep. But now the point was getting the lawyers to talk, not showing them what I knew. Letting go of that felt a bit scary. In the back of my mind, I could hear my former professor smirking that I was out of my depth."

But as she grew more experienced, Ana began to see that having answers was less important as she moved higher, while forging relationships mattered more. She says, "You can't be the expert when your domain is expansive and your span of control is broad. You need to rely on others. Plus you have less time to get up to speed on the details. The upshot is, you have to trust people and they have to trust you. And trust is built in the back-and-forth of engagement, not by knowing every last little thing."

FOUR KINDS OF POWER

Researching an earlier book, *The Web of Inclusion*, Sally spent half a day with Ted Jenkins, the fourth person hired at Intel, one of the tech giants that has made Silicon Valley a global engine of innovation. Ted had watched his company evolve from its earliest beginnings. He'd seen brilliant engineers change the world, and he'd seen brilliant engineers crash and burn.

In Ted's view, those who thrived understood that there are four kinds of power in organizations.

The first kind of power is the power of expertise, which we've been discussing. Knowledge companies like Intel (or Ashley's and Ana's employers) are entirely reliant on human talent to create, refine, prototype, manufacture, market, sell, and distribute products whose value lies in the specialized knowledge vested in their processes and design. Because expertise is required for success, demonstrating expertise can become a competitive sport in such companies. But for the reasons Ana discovered, cultivating expertise at the expense of other kinds of power will not position you as a leader.

The second kind of power is the power of connections, or the power of whom you know. Connections are usually built as you move around in the company, hold different jobs, find allies, and stay in touch. Getting to know people in your industry or sector as well as key clients and movers in your community is also important. Connections serve as a kind of currency you can use to get resources moving and assure your contributions get noticed. As Ana learned, overvaluing expertise can make you reluctant to invest time in building connections. But your relationships comprise an ever-greater part of your value as you rise.

The third kind of power is the power of personal authority or charisma, which is rooted in the confidence you inspire in others. You rarely start your career with much personal authority; it builds as your reputation develops over time. Expertise and connections can help establish personal authority, but there's always another element: a strong presence, a distinctive cast of mind, a way of speaking and listening that inspires loyalty and trust, or an unusual degree of gravitas. Personal authority is what sets the most successful leaders apart, whether or not their authority is tied to position.

The fourth kind of power is the power of position, or where you stand in the organization. Marshall likes to quote Peter Drucker, who famously observed that "the decision is always made by the person with the power to make the decision." In other words, the person who holds positional power gets to make the key decisions. This reality often infuriates experts, who believe their insights should count for more when it comes to making decisions. Perhaps they should, but they rarely do. Positional power is most effective when supported by the power of personal authority. Without it, others may not trust their leader's decisions.

Ted Jenkins noted that organizations are most healthy when all four types of power are in balance. When positional power overrides all else, decisions tend to get made arbitrarily, with insufficient information and without much support. Truly toxic organizations tend to view employees with expertise, connections, or personal authority as threats to the absolute authority of positional leaders. Jenkins noted that a chief reason Intel had been successful at drawing innovative ideas from people at every level was the value the company placed on non-positional power.

Ted Jenkins's template can be helpful if you have a history of overvaluing expertise or expecting it to translate into positional power. Expertise, connections, and personal authority are all non-positional kinds of power you can nurture and practice throughout your career. The more you develop these complementary powers, the more prepared you'll be to assume positional power.

A simple definition of *power* is "influence potential." If you want to influence the world in a positive way—as almost all of the women we have worked with want to do—you have to have power. One of our major motivations for writing this book is to help women who are already doing great work become even more influential and make even more of a positive difference in the world.

This is what happened with Ana. As her connections and confidence grew, she noticed clients and co-workers regarding her as someone they could trust. This enhanced her personal authority. When she was finally named head of her company's professional services division, she added positional power to the mix. By placing less value on expertise and getting comfortable using other kinds of power, Ana was able to move into senior management and assure her children's future.

Ana's story has resonance for many women since her rise came against so many odds. As an immigrant, she'd been the particular target of an openly chauvinistic professor who caused her to feel insecure about her engineering expertise. As the sole support of her children following her husband's early death, she was suddenly faced with the need to seek positional power in order to have sufficient income. This pushed her to get out of her comfort zone where she ended up learning that the ability to build strong relationships provided a far firmer foundation for success than the expertise she'd sought to cultivate in order to "show" her professor. By letting go of expertise, Ana was ironically finally able to feel fully confident as a leader and harness the power required to rise.

CHAPTER 8

Habit 4: Building Rather Than Leveraging Relationships

We often ask women we work with what they believe they are best at. Most cite their ability to build strong relationships, especially with clients, peers, and direct reports. Research confirms this perception. For example, in two recent global studies, senior leaders ranked their female employees most highly on motivating and engaging others, building strong teams, negotiating win-wins, empathic listening, and building morale—all skills rooted in a talent for relationships.

Yet these findings present a conundrum.

Given the consensus that many women have outstanding relationship skills, and given that organizations increasingly view the capacity to build strong relationships as a vital leadership skill, *why don't women benefit more from this strength*? Why hasn't it propelled them to ever-higher levels in their organizations? Why, when it comes to achieving top positions, do many women who are great at building relationships fail to rise?

Our experience suggests an answer.

Over the years, we've noticed that, while women are often stellar relationship builders, they tend to be less skilled at *leveraging* relationships. Or maybe not exactly less skilled, but rather noticeably reluctant to do so. Of course, this is not true of all women. We've known many who are superb at using leverage: subtle, magnetic, and strategic. These women actively enjoy building connections that benefit not only their organizations and a wide range of people, but also and very emphatically themselves.

Yet we also see talented, hardworking women who rebel at the very thought of engaging others to help them meet either specific or long-term career goals. They'll gladly spend time and energy getting to know people, offering them help, listening to their problems, giving advice, and drawing them close. But they shrink at the prospect of engaging them in a way that furthers their own ambitions.

When we ask women who are uncomfortable with the very notion of leverage what holds them back, we usually hear some variation on the following:

"I don't want others to think I'm using them."

"I want people to know I value them for themselves, not for what they can do for me."

"I don't like self-serving people and I don't want to be one."

"Basically, I'm not a hustler."

"Political games are really not my thing."

These statements make clear the underlying belief that exercising leverage translates as not being a very nice person. This is problematic because leveraging relationships is key for achieving professional success.

Most great careers are built not just on talent or hard work, but on the mutual exchange of benefits, something men are often more comfortable with than women. There's a kind of win-win horse-trading that seems to come naturally to a lot of men. They enjoy it. They're comfortable saying, *if you go to bat for me on this, I'll be there for you.* Having a close relationship with someone is often less important to them than being able to count on that person's support when they need it. This is a standard way of operating in most organizations. So women who aren't comfortable in developing win-win partnerships can put themselves at a disadvantage.

Julie Johnson, the executive coach mentioned in Chapter 2, concurs. She says, "In my observation, when men build relationships at work, they're usually very focused. They pursue people they believe can help them accomplish their objectives. Women often have multiple reasons for developing relationships. They look up to a successful peer and want her as a friend. They need someone to talk with about their work. They feel sorry for a co-worker and want to help him out. They just want people in general to like them. Or maybe they're sticking with a relationship they've outgrown in the name of loyalty."

None of these motivations (except sometimes the last) is harmful in itself, Julie points out. And building close relationships can be personally rewarding and provide emotional sustenance and support, both of which are important, especially for women who feel isolated in their jobs. But if you steadfastly refuse to leverage the relationships you've built in pursuit of your goals, you will diminish your ability to reach your full potential.

And that would be a shame. For not only will your reluctance deprive you of the help you need to act on your dreams and fulfill your talents, it will undermine your efforts to support colleagues, peer and direct reports. By restricting your sphere of influence, and taking yourself out of what you may dismiss as a distasteful political game, you will ultimately erode your capacity to make a difference in the world.

THE BASICS OF LEVERAGE

Leverage is a key career skill, a strategic way of operating that can pay outsize rewards. Successful leaders know how to employ it. They may be subtle or direct, depending on their preferred style. But if you run across someone who has real significance as a leader, you can bet he or she uses leverage every chance they get.

Even if you're uncomfortable or skeptical with the subject of leverage, you can benefit by understanding the basics of how it works. It differs from building relationships in four ways.

1. Leverage is always reciprocal, based on a quid pro quo.

The underlying premise is: *You help me and I'll help you.* This reciprocity may be stated and explicitly promised, or it may be implied and tacitly understood. But leveraged relationships always operate to mutual advantage. When you ask for something, you offer something in return, and you and the other person both continue to seek to be of service to one another.

Leverage can be the basis of a relationship, or merely an aspect of a relationship that also has a personal dimension. The point is that both people involved understand they are using one another to improve their access to resources, broaden their professional connections, and create mutually beneficial opportunities. The underlying belief is that a rising tide will lift all boats.

2. Leverage is used to achieve both tactical and strategic goals.

You initiate leverage when you make a request. Usually the request is small and specific: *I'm representing an artist whose prints are perfect for hotel lobbies. Do you know anyone in the hotel business who could introduce me to dealers who acquire work for their properties?* Or more simply: *Would you be willing to share your insights about what motivates this client?*

These are tactical favors in that they help you accomplish immediate objectives, things that would be helpful to you this week, this month, this year. Yet at its most effective, leverage also serves the larger strategic purpose of engaging those who might be helpful to you in the future. Your tactical request opens the door to a give-and-take that may not pay immediate dividends but may help you realize a long-term goal down the road. The person to whom you make the request will also view the relationship as having potential value when he or she moves to a higher level. This kind of reciprocity works best when your goals harmonize with and complement those of the people you seek to engage.

3. Leverage is highly intentional.

You establish a leveraged relationship with a specific purpose in mind, which means you use different criteria than when you establish a friendship. Does the person you seek to engage have relationships that could be useful to you, now or in the future? Does she seem poised to become more powerful over time? Is there something you're particularly well positioned to offer him now that might make him eager to be a resource for you in the future?

Liking the other person is not the primary point, though it's never a good idea to seek a reciprocal relationship with someone you dislike. That road leads to mutual exploitation, which can look a lot like leverage but has the potential to create an unholy mess. More important than how you feel about the person is how well the two of you are positioned to be useful to one another over time. This is what distinguishes leverage from friendship, though the two may overlap, and very often do.

4. Leverage brings distinctive rewards.

In the previous chapter, we looked at the difference between intrinsic and extrinsic rewards in relation to mastery and recognition. These concepts also apply to leverage. In friendship and simple colleague relations, the rewards are intrinsic, which means highly personal and subjective. You like how someone makes you feel, you enjoy his sense of humor, you're inspired or comforted after you talk to her.

In leveraged relationships, the rewards are extrinsic, which means they are measurable and concrete. You gain access to a new group of potential clients or investors. You have an opportunity to enhance your reputation and visibility or learn a new skill. In establishing leverage, your purpose is always front and center. This doesn't mean you don't respect or enjoy spending time with the other person. But the intrinsic rewards are a bonus instead of the point.

IN A GOOD CAUSE

The transactional, tactical, strategic, and intentional aspects of leverage can be a stumbling block for women. The high value women place on relationships often makes them more eager to seek out personal friendships that offer intrinsic rewards than to cultivate connections and collect chits for future use. Women who balk at using leverage often view disinterested relationships as purer, proof that you're a trustworthy and honorable person. Horse-trading may imply you have an agenda and are out for yourself.

There are two problems with this kind of thinking.

The first is that it assumes a degree of powerlessness on your part.

This is because underlying the "you help me and I'll help you" ethos is the unstated promise that *you* have the potential to be useful to the person you're engaging. You aren't just some poor soul asking for help. You're a potential resource that the other person would be fortunate to have in the years ahead.

In other words, engaging leverage is a subtle way of suggesting that you're going places. That you're a player whose help can be of value down the road. Refusing to engage in this way on the grounds that you don't want to "use" the other person suggests that you don't see yourself as having this kind of power. And that you can't imagine the other person would perceive an advantage in having a relationship with you.

The second problem with seeing leverage as a morally suspect behavior is that it reveals that familiar either/or mind-set we've been harping on in this book.

Either you're a wonderful person with pure intentions who gives no thought to your own advancement, *or* you're a conniver who uses others to achieve your own ends. *Either* you're motivated by the desire for disinterested friendship, *or* you're only out for yourself. This kind of framing allows for no middle ground, no way of being a good and helpful person who is also capable of pursuing her own self-interest.

The either/or mind-set shows itself most clearly when a woman who disdains using leverage in her career is perfectly comfortable doing so in the service of a good cause. This is quite common.

Take Amanda, a product coordinator for a manufacturer of medical devices. Amanda's company has a global reputation and takes a lot of pride in its products. Recently she was approached by one of her company's top salesmen about the hospital where she previously worked as an administrator. Amanda has kept her ties with a lot of her old colleagues, not because they're potential clients—her job is more internally facing—but because she loved the camaraderie of her old team.

She says, "Kevin asked me to introduce him to a few of the senior people I knew so he could connect with them about some of our products. I was uncomfortable with this for several reasons. I consider these people personal friends and don't want them to feel hustled. He's a real hotshot in sales and known to be pretty aggressive. Also, Kevin never showed a shred of interest in me until he found out I'd worked at that hospital. He doesn't seem to care about me as a person, so why should I set him up?"

Amanda didn't want to come right out and say no, so she tried to avoid Kevin. "I was hoping he'd get the message I wasn't interested, but he continued to call and press me. Really, the way he kept at it was pretty shameless."

Perhaps so, but that's not a great reason for Amanda to spurn the opportunity to do a simple favor for one of her company's stars, someone who is on a strong trajectory pointed up. If she wanted to protect her friends at the hospital, she could have asked them if they minded her providing the introduction. Or she could have told them to use their own judgment about whether to respond when Kevin called. And since she knows her company's products are superior, the connection could have been to her old friends' advantage. The only thing Amanda was really protecting was her own belief that asserting leverage on behalf of self-interest was an unsavory and self-interested practice.

Yet even as she was putting her nose in the air about Kevin, Amanda was forging connections and twisting arms on behalf of a domestic violence shelter that had opened in her community: calling neighbors to buy tickets to the fund-raiser and enlisting colleagues as volunteers. In taking on the cause of the women who sought refuge, Amanda was not in the least concerned that pressuring people she was friendly with was taking advantage of them or being a hustler. Because she saw the goal as worthy, she was perfectly comfortable employing the same "shameless" tactics as Kevin had. It wasn't his tactics she objected to, but employing those tactics in the pursuit of his own self-interest.

ACTING ON YOUR STRENGTH

Our experience has convinced us that leverage is a key career skill that many women could make better use of as they seek to rise. But we also recognize that the inhibitions many feel about using it are rooted in one of women's most profound and characteristic strengths.

Decades of research confirm that women's preference for building strong personal relationships instead of transactional alliances serves them as a great source of emotional fortitude, long-term resilience, and everyday joy. Women's close friendships are a boon to them, and the envy of many men, who wish they could talk more intimately with friends when they're in trouble, depressed, or feel alone.

So please don't get the idea that we're urging you to undervalue your gift for intimacy or rein in your warmth and concern for others in favor of a more leveraged approach. Instead, you might think about how to bring your skills for forging deep connections into play as you seek also to become more intentional in building relationships that may be advantageous to you in the future. This is certainly the approach taken by women who are superb at leverage, which is why their efforts can be so compelling and magnetic.

You might also examine the degree to which your dismissal of any quid pro quo element in relationships is based on a moralistic judgment. It helps to remember that leverage is a two-way street, and that even as you benefit, you are also benefitting someone else. Successful leverage is the very definition of a win-win: it's good for you and it's good for the other person. And the more genuinely others see that you're invested in the mutuality of the relationship, the more value you will create for them, and for the world.

CHAPTER 9

Habit 5: Failing to Enlist Allies from Day One

Y ou're just starting a new job. It could be with a new company or in a new division of the company you joined ten years ago. Like Ana, the Silicon Valley engineer in Chapter 7, you may be feeling a bit out of your depth. You're a novice when it comes to certain skills. You don't know how to get your hands on resources you need and aren't sure whom to ask. Your boss seems friendly and well informed, but she's in the middle of a hiring spree and you don't want to pester her with questions.

But you do need to get up to speed quickly. So you decide to focus on learning as much as you can by studying the masses of material HR has provided and immersing yourself in the details of your job. When you've got a better handle on what you're doing, you'll put your head up and start building connections.

If this is your plan, please do not proceed. You are about to make a very common mistake. It's a mistake we have both watched many talented women make, often as a consequence of overvaluing expertise (Habit 3) or being reluctant to leverage relationships (Habit 4). Sometimes it's a way of avoiding the well-known female imposter syndrome, the fear of being unmasked as unworthy or not up to the job. Sometimes you're afraid you'll be seen as a burden. Whatever the cause, it's rarely an effective approach.

Nevertheless, it persists. Women who assume new positions resolve to keep their heads down until they've mastered the details and are confident they can perform to a certain standard. They want to feel fully prepared before they start reaching out.

By contrast, men in new positions often start with the question: "Who should I connect with to make this job a success?" They view the path to success not as a matter of *what* or *how*, but of *who*. They see connections as the most important part of their job and want to start building them on day one.

The result of this who-centric approach? More support. Better positioning. Greater visibility. Less isolation.

And not incidentally, *a lot less work.*

Of course, we also see women who immediately start by building connections: successful, experienced women who know that expertise is only one source of power, and rarely the most important one. Women who recognize that getting stuck in the weeds is particularly ill-advised at the start of a job or a project, when you are most in need of support.

But it takes other women a while to figure this out, especially in companies or sectors where they've long been underrepresented. If that's your situation, you may feel awkward reaching out or skeptical that your mostly male co-workers want to get to know you. Or you may be convinced that you need to earn their respect before you even approach them.

Which path you choose will usually depend on what you

believe makes you credible at work. Is it what you do or who you're allied with? Of course it's always going to be both. If you have great connections but don't deliver, you will never inspire trust. But connections built in tandem with expertise, and from the get-go, will make for a smoother path. To be fully credible, you're always going to need allies.

Allies are peers, colleagues, higher-ups, sponsors, direct reports, and internal and external fans who support your efforts to get where you want to go. Allies know what you're trying to achieve, believe it has value, sense they have a stake in it, and do what they can to move you along. They help you find the resources you need to do a tough job. And they get the word out about your contributions.

You do the same for them because allies help each other, and mutuality lies at the root of alliance. Allies are also broadly based. People at junior levels can be valuable allies, as can those who hold frontline, support, or resource positions. The more inclusive your ally web, the more robust your support.

Allies are the heart and soul of a successful career.

Allies don't have to be friends. People with expansive and resilient webs have dozens of acquaintanceships that may last for decades without becoming personally close. Sociologists call these relationships "weak ties," and note that people are far more likely to find jobs and be rewarded for their efforts as the result of weak ties than the kind of strong ties that characterize close friendships.

Researchers find that people with a lot of loose ties or strong ally networks share two practices in common. They reach out to others first instead of waiting for others to come to them. And they go out of their way to connect people with one another—even people they don't particularly know.

Contrast this with Amanda in the previous chapter. In refusing to connect Kevin with her friends at the hospital, she cited in part that he'd never seemed to "care about her as a person." If she'd understood the power of weak ties, she wouldn't have considered this a problem. She would have known it was in her interest to enlist Kevin as an ally, regardless of his potential—or not—to be a friend, and willingly connected him with her old colleagues. She would have seen the value of drawing him into her network of connections.

ALLIES, MENTORS, AND SPONSORS

In the 1990s and early 2000s, women were exhorted to find mentors, experienced higher-ups who could offer guidance and advice. The idea became institutionalized in many organizations, with HR setting up mentoring circles or even hiring professional mentors to work with groups of women. But in 2011, the research organization Catalyst published a study that found, while mentorship could be helpful, *sponsorship* was the key success factor in women's careers.

The idea took off.

Mentors and sponsors are different in that mentors offer advice and serve as a sounding board, while sponsors are less about talk than action.

A sponsor, usually a senior leader in your organization, serves as your advocate, puts your name forward for assignments, introduces you to important colleagues, and helps remove structural road-blocks that could keep you stuck.

Obviously sponsors can be of enormous value. But there's just one problem: they're notoriously difficult to find and engage. That's because there's a huge mismatch between the number of women seeking sponsors and the number of women or men available for sponsorship. Organizational pyramids being what they are, there are just not that many people at the top.

As a woman on the executive committee of a large insurance firm remarked to Sally: "I can hardly open the door to my office without someone ambushing me about being their sponsor. There's so much emphasis on sponsorship for women but a limited number of us to go around. Plus, formal sponsorship initiatives seem to have limited success. These kinds of relationships work best when there's an element of personal chemistry. So they're most effective if they're allowed to evolve."

She added, "It's not healthy that so many women have come to believe sponsorship is the only way to move forward, a kind of magic wand that will transform their whole career. And women who haven't been able to find sponsors feel as if they've been found personally unworthy. They start blaming themselves instead of realizing it's a structural problem."

Yet most senior women managed to get where they are without a sponsor to help them, as the insurance executive points out. "Speaking for myself, it would have been wonderful to have someone powerful in the company in my corner, but twenty-five years ago nobody ever heard of women having that kind of support, at least not in this company. There were only senior male executives and the fair-haired boys they chose to promote, otherwise known as the old boys' network."

Sponsors are a valuable kind of ally, but they're only one kind. So if you're struggling to find one, your best response might be to pour that energy into building a broad ally network instead. This will not only strengthen you, it will increase the likelihood that you'll find a sponsor by giving you more visibility and assuring your contributions get more widely known.

Sheryl Sandberg, who has no doubt been inundated with sponsor requests for several decades during her rise at Google and then Facebook, writes in her book *Lean In* that potential sponsors are most likely to be attracted to people who already have a lot of support. In her view, sponsors are motivated to expend effort on behalf of those they see as already on a path to success rather than those hoping for rescue or waiting for someone to notice them. And one of the ways you signal you're on that path is by actively building up your web of connections.

In its original report, Catalyst also noted that sponsorship is most effective when it's been earned. As the authors observed: "To attract sponsors, employees need to make their skills, strengths, and work known to colleagues as well as to senior leaders. They must build reputations as flexible, collegial professionals who are consistently committed to their own career development."

How do you do this? By actively engaging allies.

Preferably from the day you start a new job.

THE AMBASSADOR

Dianna, a trademark litigator for a mineral conglomerate headquartered in Melbourne, Australia, has always been diligent about building connections. As a result, she attracted an excellent sponsor who was instrumental in landing Dianna a stretch assignment in Singapore, where she was hired to lead the legal team in the company's large and profitable shipping division.

Dianna says, "I arrived knowing nothing about maritime law, which is extremely complex and could not be more different from what I'd been doing. Needless to say, I felt a bit overwhelmed. I told my boss I intended to spend every waking hour getting up to speed on our practice, but that was not at all what he wanted to hear."

Her boss told Dianna he had not hired her because he needed another excellent maritime lawyer. "He said the guys he had were extremely knowledgeable. But they had a long history of squabbling among themselves, withholding information from one another, and generally alienating our clients. I'd led a couple of successful teams in my former job and he wanted me to do the same here. His exact words were: 'You wouldn't be here if you weren't a good lawyer, but you're not here to be a good lawyer. You're here to be a leader. That's your job.'"

Dianna knew she had to start forging relationships but quickly realized that the worst place to start doing so was with her team. She says, "From the first meeting, the guys made clear they saw me as an unqualified outsider who'd been parachuted in by headquarters to take a job one of them deserved. The fact that I was a woman certainly didn't help—it was an incredibly macho culture. They had exactly zero interest in seeing me succeed, and you could cut the resentment with a knife. All I could do was be pleasant and not let them push me around. Trying to get buddy-buddy with them would have been a disaster."

Instead, Dianna began reaching out to people in operations who could help her access information and get resources flowing, and to customers and suppliers that her team had long ignored. She says, "At first I felt self-conscious because I was so behind the curve in terms of maritime practice, but I decided honesty was the best policy. I prepared for every encounter by making lists of questions. Being a lawyer by training, I was used to providing *answers*, so this was a new behavior for me. But it taught me to take risks and be more open. And of course I learned a lot."

Once she had the lay of the land, Dianna began joining regional trade groups, immersing herself in Singapore's rich maritime culture. After a few events, she realized that a number of connections from her previous job could be helpful to people she was meeting, especially clients looking to expand their trading portfolios.

She says, "I was surprised to find that the network I'd built in Australia gave me currency I could use in the shipping world. Also, internal people began seeing me as a way to build up their own connections at headquarters. Without intending it, I became a kind of ambassador for our company in Singapore. This gave me a lot of visibility and strength."

As Dianna's web expanded, she began sharing resources and connections with members of her team. "We'd be in a meeting and someone would bring up a problem. Instead of trying to provide an answer, I'd say, 'I think Joe in operations could help you with that. I'll give him a call after this meeting.' Or, 'I happen to know a customer in Mumbai who would love your suggestion.' Sharing contacts like this was really useful because, like most dysfunctional teams, the people I worked with were very inward-looking. Once they saw I could help them, they loosened up. I knew I'd made it when two of the guys who'd most resented me began soliciting my advice on a project."

Now a corporate officer in Melbourne, Dianna looks on her

years in Singapore as the turning point in her career. "Instead of seeing myself as a smart lawyer who scored points based on my knowledge of the law, I began to see myself as a leader who brought out the best in people and could help them connect across continents. I'd never be where I am now if I hadn't been forced to recognize that alliances are more important than what you know."

ALLIES ARE YOUR BRAND

Ever since Tom Peters's iconic *Fast Company* cover story, "The Brand Called You," was published in 1997, people have understood the importance of building a distinctive personal brand. When you think about your brand, you may think in terms of your skills, your reputation, and how you present yourself. These elements all comprise your brand. But as Dianna learned when she stepped into her ambassador role in Singapore, your alliances are part of your brand as well.

Effective personal marketers understand this. They know that alliances and connections establish them as potential leaders. This is why they can mention the names of colleagues without any discomfort. And feel happy that their colleagues are doing the same.

Name-dropping gets a bad rap, but it's really only a problem if you're tenuously (or not at all) connected to the people you claim to know. If these people *are* in your orbit, sharing that information is not only a great way to enhance your brand, but a powerful means of building credibility. You are known by the company you keep. You are also talking about them in a way that helps them!

Alliances have always been a big part of Marshall's brand as an executive coach, author, and thought leader because having powerful people vouch for you is the best way to establish yourself in a competitive marketplace. As a coach, Marshall makes no bones about the simplicity of his technique, which is based on a few very straightforward steps: asking for feedback, thanking, following up, advertising, and feedforward (as you will see in Chapter 19). Given this simplicity, how has he built a client base that includes the most high-profile CEOs in the world? By positively using the power of his connections to build his credibility as a coach and help his clients help one another.

These connections include his clients. For while many coaches keep their client lists private, Marshall only works with clients who are willing to openly discuss the fact that they have a coach.

Marshall always notes that he has learned more from his clients than they have learned from him. He is very proud of his clients—and they are more than happy to help him. For example, his book *Triggers* was endorsed by twenty-seven major CEOs. This is a great source of pride for Marshall. Why? Because thirty years ago, almost no CEO would admit to having a coach—they would have found it to be a sign of weakness. Today, smart CEOs are happy to have a coach—and willing to talk about it.

Marshall regularly has his clients meet for dinner and discuss how they can help each other. He is very comfortable with the fact that his clients often learn more from one another than they learn from him. This type of win-win collaboration is good for all of the participants.

This strategy has multiple benefits: It establishes his clients as part of an elite group of learners. It gives them other people who are at the top to talk to, a scarce resource at the highest levels. It creates potential business relationships. It enhances everyone's public profile. And it builds Marshall's reputation as the coach with the A-plus list of clients.

You can use a version of this approach, starting where you are and using what you have and whoever you know.

When you enlist allies on a project, be sure to talk about them in a positive way. Praise what they're doing and connect them with others. You don't need to be the world's biggest extrovert to do this. You don't need to try to make friends or form close ties. You just need to engage as many people as possible in your efforts to have an impact. And you want to do it in a public way so that you, and they, can benefit from the association.

The ideal time to do this is when you're starting a new job. It will bring you support and establish your credibility faster than anything else you might try. But it's also a useful technique if you've been in your job for a while. Ask yourself: What do you want your next step here to be? What project would you like to be involved in? Then identify five people who could be helpful and start telling them what you want to do.

You might say, "Carol, I'd like to expand my client base in the western suburbs. Do you know anyone I might contact? I'll let them know how well your team is doing." Or: "Ben, I heard you signed up that great comedy act that performed at our last retreat. Could you let me know how you found them? I'm planning an event for my professional network. Maybe you'd like to come?"

These are tiny asks and offers, but that's not the point. The idea is to start pulling people into your network by asking and returning small favors. A willingness to trade favors and form alliances is the lifeblood of a successful career. So you'll want to get comfortable reaching out at the first opportunity.

CHAPTER 10

Habit 6: Putting Your Job Before Your Career

We frequently work with smart, talented, hardworking women who quickly ascend to a certain level and then remain there for an unusually long time. These women often rationalize their situation, citing things they like about their jobs, such as the comfort of long-term relationships and being able to use skills they've had a chance to hone.

But deep down, many of them feel frustrated. They watch colleagues who entered the company in the same year they did sail past them. They see someone *they* hired snag a high-profile job they'd hoped for. They watch their salary increase by tiny increments despite outstanding performance, because their company's policies peg salary to position.

If you find yourself stuck like this, you may have devoted so much time and energy to doing your job superbly that you've neglected to take the steps needed to propel you to the next level. Maybe you haven't built the visibility and connections you need to create a demand for your skills. Maybe you've sent so many signals that you enjoy being where you are that people no longer think of your name when a higher-level position opens up.

If this describes you, you're probably focusing on your job at the expense of your career. You're looking at what's on your plate now instead of seeing the big picture. You're sacrificing your long-term prospects on the altar of today.

Of course, you may love your job and feel it's a great fit, so your reluctance is understandable. But remaining stuck is never a good idea. Staying in the same job too long undermines your long-term satisfaction and feelings of self-worth. It diminishes your ability to have an impact, as well as your earning potential. It sidelines you and sends a message that you don't believe you deserve better.

Why does this happen so often with women? Is there an underlying reason? Of course, your organization may be more challenging for you than for men who fit the boss's image of a real up-and-comer. But often there's something else at play. Perhaps you feel undecided about what you really want to do and let your uncertainty paralyze your ability to act. Or maybe you're temperamentally averse to risk.

But in our experience, the most common reason women put their job before their career is rooted in one of their greatest virtues: loyalty.

Research shows that loyalty is a primary reason women tend to stay in their jobs longer than men. It's a virtue that can easily become a trap. The desire to be loyal can lead you to neglect your future, sacrifice your ambitions, and sell your talent and potential short. Others may benefit, but you do not.

PERSONAL LOYALTY

Sally met Serena at a point when Serena's dissatisfaction had finally surfaced and inspired her to try a new approach. She had spent eleven years as a senior production assistant for a network news show based in LA, which qualifies as an unusually long time to stay in such a job in her business.

The producer Serena worked for had won a notable number of Emmys, and she had always felt proud to work for him. She loved the fact that he constantly praised her contributions and talked about how lucky he was to have someone with her talent and experience working for him. He had even called her out for special thanks when he won his most recent Emmy, which thrilled her parents, immigrants from Egypt who enjoy watching American awards shows and were ecstatic to hear their daughter's name mentioned on network TV.

Serena liked the day-to-day rhythm of her job, valued her leadership role on the team, and felt she benefited from her boss's prestige. But remaining a senior PA for so long had provided its share of painful moments. She says, "A male assistant who joined when I did took off like a rocket, becoming a producer after just five years. He was no better at his job than I was, but he was constantly on the lookout for opportunities. I *waited* for opportunities, figuring my boss and senior management would know when I was ready to move up."

Attending a leadership retreat for media professionals from diverse backgrounds provided Serena with her wake-up call. The program focused on career development. Participating in the workshops and getting individual coaching helped her see that she needed to start thinking long-term or she could end up being a PA for the rest of her life.

The experience also forced Serena to confront the role she'd played in keeping herself where she was. Like many women, she'd always taken the just-work-hard approach, attending to what needed to be done that day, that week, or that month. She says, "I knew I wanted to produce, but I always figured that when the time was right, it would happen. That retreat made clear that my approach wasn't working. I needed a different plan."

As she considered how to take action, Serena realized her first task had to be letting people at the network know she was ready for a challenge. But the thought of doing so stirred up strong feelings that gave her a clue to the fears that had held her back. "Just the idea of telling my boss I wanted his support in becoming a producer basically filled me with dread. I was afraid he'd see me as disloyal for leaving him in the lurch. I was afraid he'd think I'd just been using my position with him as a stepping-stone. As if standing on the same stone for eleven years wasn't enough!"

The more she thought about it, the more Serena realized that her sense of loyalty was keeping her stuck. Because she felt grateful to her boss, she had never pushed for another position. And while he had never exploited her, Serena's passivity had benefited him at every turn.

Serena also realized that, although her boss had always been lavish in praising her, he mostly did so to staff and other producers. He'd never raved about her work to the senior network people in New York. Yet they were the ones who needed to know what she was capable of if she had any expectation of moving on.

"Why wouldn't he have talked to them about me?" she wondered. "Partly because I'd never asked him to. But maybe the other reason was that I'd made myself indispensable to him over the years. So why *would* he have taken the initiative to help me move on? Don't get me wrong, I'm not saying my still being a PA was his fault. I did it to myself. But I needed to get over my attachment to being seen as totally loyal if I wanted to become a producer."

Some of Serena's resistance had to do with family. She knew her parents would never understand her wanting to move higher, not only because they idolized her boss but because they came from a culture in which anyone who managed to land a decent job hung on to it forever. "In Egypt, you were lucky to have any job, so you proved yourself worthy by being fanatically loyal. If you weren't, you were seen as arrogant and irresponsible to your family."

Once Serena understood that loyalty had been the chief factor in keeping her trapped, she was able to approach her boss about her desire to move ahead. He was immediately cooperative, and within months she was producing a series of documentaries in New York. "I was so worried he'd think I was disloyal," she reflects. "But most jobs *are* stepping-stones on the way to something else. And I've come to realize there's no shame in using where you are to position yourself for what you want next. Of course he understood that. How could he not? That's what he did, or he wouldn't have gotten to where he was."

TEAM LOYALTY

Serena was loyal to her boss. But we often come across women who sacrifice their ambitions because of loyalty to their team or unit. Carlos Marin, an executive coach who works extensively in Latin America as well as the United States, finds overcommitment to their team to be the primary reason women fail to invest in their own careers.

Carlos says, "Many women I work with get very involved with nurturing their team and spend huge amounts of time with their people. This is great for their people, and it can provide intrinsic rewards for the women. But it doesn't necessarily serve them to be so internally focused."

That's because, in Carlos's view, their devotion to their teams can cause highly accomplished women to neglect building the networks with senior leaders and external partners they need to advance. "So while their male colleagues are building relationships that will help them in the future, the women are spending all their waking hours managing their teams. They appear to enjoy it, and it certainly pays off in terms of their team's performance, but it does not get the women where they want to go."

Not only are these women failing to build the relationships that could position them for the future, they're actively honing and advertising a skill that identifies them as suited for a less than senior level. As Carlos points out, "Managing a team superbly ultimately proves you have great skills as a manager. But building strong outside networks is a *promotional* skill aimed at getting recognition for the larger organization. So while women are honing their management skills and sending the message that they're wonderful managers, their male colleagues are busy building promotional skills and sending the message that they're terrific promoters."

This matters because top leadership roles tend to be more about potential for the next level of responsibility than management of the current level of responsibility, a reality often misunderstood at managerial levels. As Carlos observes, "Senior executives succeed by extending external relationships in a way that serves the larger organization. They also deal with the board on big-picture strategic issues. They do not succeed by only being great managers of internal people."

The upshot is that if, out of loyalty to your team, you allow your energy to be consumed by conscientiously tending to its needs, you will primarily prove that you are superbly suited for remaining in an internally facing position. The management skills that have gotten you here will end up keeping you here, instead of helping you rise to a place where you could have maximum impact.

HEALTHY SELF-INTEREST

In addition to realizing that her loyalty to her boss was keeping her trapped, Serena became aware of another vulnerability. She says, "I had this incredible fear of appearing, or of *being*, self-serving. I kept remembering the guy who made producer after just five years. He talked about nothing except producing. He was a production assistant, but he introduced himself as a producer! At the time I thought it was pompous and showed he was out for himself. But now I think, what's so terrible about looking out for your own interests?"

Women are frequently uncomfortable admitting self-interest, not only to others but also to themselves. This can keep you focused on your job instead of your career. By contrast, thinking in terms of career development suggests that you view every job or project as a way of positioning yourself for what might come next.

This doesn't mean you only think about the future instead of appreciating where you are now. But it does mean you assess the value of every job not just in terms of how much you enjoy it or how valued you are, but also in terms of how it could serve your long-term self-interest.

There's nothing wrong with this. In fact, it's just being smart. After all, what defines self-interest in the workplace? Ultimately, it's being able to create the conditions for building a career that gives full scope to your talents while providing you with the means to build a life that feels satisfying and worthwhile. You exercise this self-interest by pursuing jobs that maximize your potential to achieve these goals. Not just now, but over the span of your working life.

Of course, your definition of self-interest may not be the same as someone else's. Maybe you value time more than money. Maybe time with your family is paramount. Maybe you want a career that offers variety or the chance to travel or brings you into contact with people you admire. Or one that provides financial independence. Whatever it is, knowing what inspires you and working intentionally to create it requires that you acknowledge and then act upon your self-interest.

Self-interest doesn't seem to be a problem for many of the men we work with. Men usually like the idea of winning, so they're comfortable putting their interests and those of their family first. Some women do this, but others seem to think that pursuing their self-interest will make them a bad person.

Heidi is an analyst for a global financial corporation. She's seen as brilliant, but her career had stalled when Marshall was brought in as her coach. In their first meeting, he asked what she thought might be her problem.

"The first thing you need to know," said Heidi, "is that I'm not like a lot of the guys here. They never think about the bank. They think about themselves, what they can get out of working here. They're up front about it, so they spend more time angling for promotions than doing their jobs. That's not my way. Delivering the best work I can is more important to me than schmoozing or playing politics. I think more about this institution than I do about my own career."

She paused for a moment, then added thoughtfully, "Maybe that's my problem?"

Marshall had to agree.

He said, "Here's how I see it. This bank is doing well because it's very good at investing people's money. The bank is highly ethical, which is great, but it is not curing cancer! I think that you should do your best to help the bank. You should also do your best to have a great career and a great life. As long as you're not doing anything immoral, unethical, or illegal, you don't need to sacrifice your future for the bank. And who are you to judge other people here and decide they are lesser human beings because they, along with helping the bank, are interested in helping themselves and their families?"

Marshall's words startled Heidi. But over the next few months, she began to view her desire to demonstrate loyalty to her institution and disdain for her own self-interest in a different light. Maybe her self-righteous insistence that she didn't want to "play the game" was in fact a clever way of keeping herself stuck.

She began asking herself what she was really trying to achieve. Why was she at the bank? What kept her in her job? And where did she ultimately want it to lead her? If her values were so at odds with the demands of her profession, would she be better off at a nonprofit? Or was she simply trying to deny the very real satisfaction she took in her work as an analyst?

Pondering these questions forced Heidi to realize that her judgments about the people she worked with only served to alienate her and make her feel misunderstood. To be honest, she *enjoyed* using her extraordinary analytic skills and insights. She loved the intellectual challenge. And she felt a guilty pleasure when she bested her colleagues.

Why guilty? Probably because her mother had always admonished her that being competitive was "unbecoming" in a girl. She didn't agree with her mother, then or now, but she was behaving as if she did.

Once she figured this out, Heidi was able to admit that she liked being really good at her work, and that bailing on her job to pursue something different was a self-sabotaging idea. She simply needed to let go of the sense of guilt, instilled in her from childhood, that held her back from realizing her full potential. She needed, in Sheryl Sandberg's phrase, to *lean in*.

So if you're stuck in the loyalty trap, or have a problem admitting self-interest, or if you make a big point of disdaining the politics you see other people play, you can benefit by considering how well these attitudes really serve you, how suited they are for getting you where you want to go. Women who use their jobs as a way to avoid thinking about their careers often have a problem admitting to ambition. But the world needs ambitious women— why not you?

CHAPTER 11

Habit 7: The Perfection Trap

Striving to be perfect may have helped get you where you are, but it will get in your way as you aspire to higher levels. There are many reasons this is so.

- Striving to be perfect creates stress, for you and for those around you, because it's based on expectations that human beings may occasionally live up to but which cannot be sustained over time.
- Striving to be perfect keeps you riveted on details, distracting you from the big-picture orientation that's expected when you reach a senior position.
- Striving to be perfect creates a negative mind-set in which you're bothered by every little thing that goes wrong, since even a small mistake can "ruin" the whole. And negativity is never valued in a leader.
- Striving to be perfect sets you up for disappointment for the simple reason that it's unrealistic. You, and the people who work with and for you, will never be perfect—at least as long as you live on planet earth.

In our experience, women are especially vulnerable to the perfection trap, the belief that they will succeed if they do their job perfectly and never mess anything up. While women in general tend to be seen as better leaders than men, they are often undermined by their tendency to give themselves a hard time, a habit rooted in the desire to be perfect. The result is that even high-achieving women tend to take failures deeply to heart, get tangled up in self-blame, and stew over mistakes instead of moving on.

Other coaches and practitioners we work with share this assessment. Julie Johnson, the executive coach quoted in Chapter 8, finds that the desire to be perfect is one of the two most serious challenges facing the women she works with. (You'll read about the other one in the next chapter.) This has not changed during her thirty years in the field. Yet she rarely sees perfectionism among her male clients.

WHY WOMEN?

Why are women often vulnerable to this desire to be perfect? Or to the belief that if they're not perfect, they are somehow unworthy? Experience and research suggest two reasons: gender expectations that start in childhood, and how those expectations get reinforced in the workplace.

Girls tend to be rewarded for being obedient daughters and excellent students, while boys are given more latitude. People will often speak fondly about a naughty little boy. He's considered charming, amusing, and adorable. That's especially true if he's good at sports, where cutting corners and showboating is routinely rewarded, along with bending the rules in order to score points.

By contrast, girls who fail to conform to expected standards don't get much of a break. Schools are far more likely to penalize girls for acting out and for aggressive behaviors such as fighting. With boys, these behaviors are often dismissed as a testosterone spurt, but they're viewed as disgraceful in girls. These attitudes often prevail even in families and schools committed to gender equality.

Such expectations can prompt girls to seek approval by striving to get everything right, avoiding mistakes and dotting every *i*. In other words, by trying to be perfect. Girls consistently average higher grades than boys, in part because they develop earlier but also in part because doing so is the surest way to earn approval. It's not that boys don't get rewarded for good grades, but the boys who receive the most praise are usually the sports stars. As athletes, they are expected to be assertive, show confidence, stand out from the pack, and be bold. After all, a Hail Mary pass is admired even when it fails to hit its intended receiver. What's the greatest praise an athlete can receive? That he *dominated*. Valedictorians are never described in those terms.

Executive coach Carlos Marin, quoted in the previous chapter, observes a similar pattern in organizations. "Coaching data and the psychometric surveys we deliver when doing assessments suggest that men at the executive level are most likely to be rewarded for daring and risk-taking," he says. "Women at similar levels are most likely to be rewarded for precision and correctness."

The upshot is that many of the senior women Carlos and his

team work with internalize the expectation that they should be conscientious and precise. He notes that this can result in an excessive fear of making mistakes that shows up in all sorts of ways. "For example, even in high-stakes executive team meetings, men tend to be comfortable making statements they haven't necessarily thought through, or even stupid statements. But if a woman says something stupid, she'll be consumed by embarrassment, even shame, and have a hard time letting it go. She might decide to avoid this by keeping her mouth shut in the future. And then she'll be criticized for being too cautious or not contributing."

The fear of making mistakes is of course compounded by the fact that, as a woman, your mistakes are often viewed more critically in male organizational cultures. Your errors may be seized on as proof that women in general can't make the grade, which can affect how other women in the company are viewed. This compounds the guilt you feel over having made a mistake—and over not being perfect.

The process is intensified if you're a member of a minority. In the United States, African American women often feel the burden of carrying the expectations of their entire community on their shoulders, as do immigrants from many cultures in Europe, North America, and Asia. Women in India, at home and abroad, may feel pressure not just to be the perfect employee and high performer, but the perfect daughter-in-law, constantly trying to appease a family that is skeptical of her every move. If you're in one of these situations, learning to let go of the desire to be perfect assumes a special urgency lest you sink under the weight of expectations.

In order to rise, you have to lay your burden down.

THE COST

Carlos Marin notes that people who set very high standards for themselves usually set very high standards for others. This can make co-workers and direct reports feel resentful. So while it's understandable that a woman might believe that being perfect is her only path to success, her strenuous efforts will often come back to bite her.

Take the case of Vera, a super-high performer at a global insurance company headquartered in northern Europe. Vera is an intellectual powerhouse, extraordinarily hardworking, and superbly organized. She speaks five languages, is an outstanding public speaker, and has scored major successes in both operations and finance. All of this made her a natural candidate for CEO of her company, but her perfectionism ended up undermining her when she was scouted for the job.

Her vulnerability surfaced when her company began soliciting feedback on its three top candidates. It turned out that people she worked with, while they respected her work ethic and were generally in awe of her achievements, often found her overcontrolling and judgmental.

One close colleague wrote: "Vera is an amazing performer and unsparing in her dedication. But she tends to ask too much of people. She's so worried about failure that she ends up micromanaging her team and driving us to exhaustion."

Another reported: "It's impossible to be relaxed around Vera because she's always nervous that something will go wrong. As a result, her meetings feel totally scripted. Nobody wants to throw out some bright idea that hasn't already been fully vetted because she'll find five ways it could end in disaster. That limits creativity in her division. People meet their performance objectives, but you don't see a lot of innovation, even though the people in her unit are exceptionally smart."

In addition to alienating co-workers, Vera's perfectionism has made her reluctant to take risks. Sweating the small stuff usually has this effect. If you're trying to be perfect, every task or encounter feels high stakes. You're always on the lookout for something to go wrong since even the smallest glitch has the power to undermine your perfect image.

Risk-taking requires being open to failure. While risk must be thoughtfully assessed, the outcome is never assured or entirely within your control. The desire to be perfect, by contrast, keeps you focused on what you *can* control. This narrows your horizons and demonstrates insecurity instead of the confidence in the future that being an effective leader requires.

In the end, risk aversion was the chief reason Vera was bypassed for the CEO position. She had remarkable talents, but at the highest executive level, where big decisions about the future need to be made, some degree of risk-taking is essential if the organization is to evolve and grow. A board member involved in the search summed it up: "Vera is brilliant at dealing with situations where potential difficulties can be seen and known. But what worked in the past doesn't help you build the future. For that, you need a healthy ability to trust, willingness to take considered risks, and a big vision of what the organization could become."

THE HEALTHY PERFECTIONIST

Of course, the drive to deliver superb results is an enormous asset so long as your perfectionistic tendencies can be curbed. As an example, coach Julie Johnson points to one of her clients, Dana, whom she describes as a healthy perfectionist. Dana has spent the last eighteen years on the executive committee of an international transport company and is considered the coolest head in the room by her CEO.

Julie describes what makes Dana different from other perfectionists. She says, "Dana has very high standards but she's learned not to be controlling. She knows that people are human and make mistakes. She doesn't focus on the one little thing that went wrong and judge the whole based on that. She *notices* the detail, but considers it in a larger context. She's a perfectionist by nature, a detail person for sure, but she has a broad perspective and is very tolerant with people. She works incredibly hard but is often the first to let go when things don't turn out as planned. And she has a great sense of humor so she can handle criticism and put people at ease. It all comes down to her being a confident person."

Julie notes that Dana has two skills most perfectionists lack. She's good at delegating and she knows how to prioritize.

Perfectionists usually struggle with delegation. If you have super-exacting standards, it stands to reason that you would have difficulty letting others do their jobs. And because monitoring people's efforts is time-consuming and often fraught, you just may decide that it's easier and quicker to do the job yourself.

The upshot is that you end up loading extra tasks onto your already-too-full plate. You involve yourself in phone calls you have no need to be on or proof preliminary drafts of reports that someone else is in charge of. If you make such interventions a habit, your team will get used to having every step of their performance checked, so they'll become less diligent about preparation. After all, why should they put in a lot of effort when you're going to end up inserting yourself at every stage of the process?

By rushing in, you take away their incentive to perform, to learn, to grow, and to get better. This is how dysfunctional teams are born.

And if you struggle with delegation at work, you may also find it difficult at home. You take up the slack for your kids when they neglect their chores or "forget" to tell you about after-school events that require special transportation. Like your co-workers, your kids come to expect your intervention and get accustomed to the idea that they don't need to take responsibility.

If this describes you, you might consider whether you are enabling those around you to be helpless, which is what people who fail to delegate often do. If this is your pattern at work *and* at home, you may end up expiring from the stress or becoming trapped in a resentful martyrdom.

Willingness to delegate becomes ever more important as you move to higher levels. You have more people to manage, more of whom have specialized skills and knowledge. If you try to do their jobs for them, you'll be eaten alive. So if "it's easier to do it myself" is your go-to response, you might want to consider that you are undermining your potential as a leader, as well as taking on a lot of extra work.

A root cause of the failure to delegate is often an inability to prioritize, to decide what's important and what doesn't require your attention. If you're trying to be perfect, you're going to struggle with prioritizing because you're only comfortable when *everything* is right. So you may treat being two minutes late for a meeting as seriously as missing the filing date for a finance report since both undermine your need to demonstrate perfection.

If you have perfectionist tendencies, you can best serve your long-term interests by learning to delegate, prioritize, and get comfortable taking measured risks. This will create a less stressful environment—for you and for others—and demonstrate your readiness to move forward. The good news is that you will be the primary beneficiary if you lay your burden down.

But only if you can accept not being perfect.

CHAPTER 12

Habit 8: The Disease to Please

Trying to be a perfect person is a trap, given human limitations. But trying to be a wonderful person can be a trap as well. The desire to be wonderful in all circumstances—to be thoughtful and nice and make everyone around you feel good—is known among coaches as "the disease to please." It's considered particularly prevalent among women.

If you're a chronic pleaser, chances are you know it. You may even talk about it, usually in an apologetic tone. And you are probably aware of how it holds you back. Maybe you routinely say yes to tasks and jobs that you know will eat up your time but bring you little benefit. Maybe you spend hours commiserating with people who seem to enjoy complaining, and then wonder what you do to attract them. Maybe you get enmeshed with colleagues who have a knack for creating dramas, and whom others seem to skillfully avoid. You resolve to keep away from them, but end up getting sucked into their toxic orbit.

The disease to please can undermine your ability to make clear decisions because you're always trying to split the difference among competing needs in hopes of creating consensus or avoiding giving offense. This can impair your judgment and leave you vulnerable to manipulation by people who know how to use guilt to get others to accommodate their needs. It can rob you of the capacity to act with authority for fear of disappointing others or making them even temporarily unhappy. It can make you an unreliable advocate or ally because you are so easily swayed. It can distract you from your purpose, squander your time and talents, and contribute to your general stuckness.

The disease to please is anything but pleasant and it can be positively poisonous for your career. But what makes you this way? And how can you break the habit?

Like perfectionists, chronic pleasers usually have difficulty delegating. Perfectionists resist it because they believe they can do everything better, while pleasers are motivated by the desire to be helpful and a reluctance to burden others or let down anyone who might have relied on them in the past.

You may be aware of all these drawbacks, yet still find yourself hooked on pleasing because the effort you put into being helpful and putting others first makes you feel like a good person.

Certainly there are men who find themselves in these no-win situations. But psychologists and coaches will tell you that the disease to please is more typically found in women.

Why?

The answer is probably a combination of factors. As already noted, research shows that girls are more likely to be rewarded for being obedient, agreeable, helpful to others, and "nice," both at home and at school. And organizations often shepherd entry- and mid-level women into "helping positions," where they're judged on their ability to meet the needs of others and may be penalized for self-assertion. Also, as we saw in the previous chapter, even women at senior levels tend to be most highly rewarded when they fulfill expectations and act in ways that others find pleasing rather than when they act boldly or assert independent views.

Pleasing also gives women the opportunity to use the nurturing and intuitive strengths that they have developed over millennia of evolution and upon which their families depend. These include sensitivity to human interaction and a gift for noticing when others are upset, worried, frightened, or tuned out. These are skills many women hone over a lifetime, skills that get a special workout if you become a mother.

Obviously, these skills provide many advantages, not only at home but also at work. The ability to read the needs of others gives you an edge when it comes to motivating, engaging, and communicating with customers, clients, peers, and direct reports. It can be of great benefit to your organization and your customers, especially as hearts-and-minds engagement becomes an ever-more-critical component of success.

Yet when the need to be liked or perceived as helpful overwhelms other considerations, the skills that should provide an advantage can prove detrimental. And while the need to please may serve you in the earlier stages of your career, it will impede you as you move higher, eroding your capacity to demonstrate leadership and serving as the ultimate tool for giving your power away.

THE LINCHPIN

Nancy is a senior administrator at a highly rated regional medical center. She started her career as a receptionist with only two years of community college. No one in her family had gone beyond high school, and she had never envisioned herself in management. But she's smart, efficient, very hardworking, and remarkably warm and cheerful. Soon after she started, medical teams began relying on her to coordinate with patients.

Patients loved her, and the center soon began receiving notes about how much Nancy had helped them. Community ratings for the center began to rise. Then a local philanthropist made a stunningly large donation because his mother had been so well treated by Nancy. After two years, senior staff decided she was wasting her time with reception duties. They created a patient advocate position for her, and pointed her to a free tuition program where she earned a four-year degree in hospital administration.

Nancy rose steadily through the ranks. She was asked to start an outreach initiative for families of patients with serious chronic disease to involve them in proactively managing care. She created a highly visible community engagement program that raised the center's regional profile. She helped develop patient-service training for medical professionals that received national recognition. When the medical center was acquired by a larger system, many of its programs were consolidated, but Nancy's innovations were adapted by the larger system, which viewed them as a fundraising advantage.

For twenty years, Nancy flourished. Said a colleague, "Anything we did that was outward-facing, it was always 'let's bring in Nancy.' She was our go-to for getting outside people involved." By her late thirties, Nancy was head of external affairs for the entire system, with patient services given a high priority and folded into her brief.

But upon reaching this pinnacle, Nancy began to hit some bumps.

Put simply, she was spread too thin, in part because her new portfolio was so broad, but also because she was still enmeshed in previous responsibilities. Patients and families she had worked with in the past continued to call on her for help. Nurses and doctors sometimes asked her to run interference when they encountered roadblocks.

A nurse-manager noted, "Nancy's always had this magic touch, a way of calming nervous and distraught people. Staff found it easier to bring her in than to try to deal with difficult situations themselves. They saw her as the linchpin for when things got rough." Community groups also preferred to deal with Nancy rather than the new people she had hired for the job. She found herself agreeing to a crowded schedule of public events.

Nancy says, "I felt like I had five jobs, and it was running me into the ground. But I didn't really see a good way out. I knew I should focus on the job I had, but so many people had come to rely on me that I didn't feel right letting them down. I knew patient and family histories and problems. I knew the pain people were in, physical and mental. How could I say I was too busy to help? How could I tell them I'd become a big shot who didn't have time for their problems? They trusted me and saw me as a friend."

As Nancy struggled to meet so many responsibilities, her staff began to question her approach. Some felt marginalized and viewed her as always swooping in to do their jobs. And despite her efforts, a number of high-profile patients who were accustomed to her being there for them sensed she was drawing away and grew resentful. Her attempts to please everyone were failing. She felt like nothing she could do was ever enough.

ENTER ILSA

A board member who had known Nancy for over a decade recommended the system hire a coach who could help her figure
things out. Ilsa had worked with dozens of women and quickly
saw Nancy's problem: a need to be liked and viewed as caring and
giving by virtually everyone she met.

"I've seen this so often," says Ilsa. "Pleasing often works for
women until they reach a certain level. Then suddenly it seriously
does not. When you're in charge of a lot of people, you need to
set expectations. If you don't, you're virtually training the people
who work for you to rely on you."

Ilsa noted a number of factors at work in Nancy's dilemma, all
of them common among chronic pleasers. First up was Nancy's
pervasive sense of guilt. She felt self-conscious about going beyond
her family's expectations, and feared being seen as "too big for her
britches," a typical complaint in her family about anyone who was
successful. As a result, Nancy was constantly trying to prove she
didn't think she was better than anyone else. This made it almost
impossible for her to say no.

"Nancy believed that if she left any of the people she had
worked with behind, she would be seen as callous and only out for
herself," says Ilsa. "That kind of judgment felt intolerable to her,
so she kept trying to meet everyone's expectations. The problem
was, her expanded responsibilities didn't leave time or scope to do
that. But rather than accept this and risk being seen as successful
and therefore—as her family saw it—a snob, she continually let
her boundaries be violated."

Ilsa also noted Nancy's excessive fear of gossip. "She couldn't stand the thought that people might be talking about her in a negative way. She knew the hospital was a gossip mill. Lots of workplaces are, especially those with rigid hierarchical structures, which certainly describes a hospital environment. People *do* get talked about, especially people in high positions who have moved quickly through the ranks."

Nancy, however, imagined she could remain immune from sniping by being everyone's best friend. Many chronic pleasers share this illusion. Says Ilsa, "Being liked was so important to Nancy that it was hard for her to accept she could not control what other people said about her. But as a senior administrator, she couldn't avoid stirring up some resentment. It comes with the territory, no matter how nice you try to be. You have to make peace with that if you're in a leadership position. Otherwise you'll be at everyone's beck and call."

Ilsa helped Nancy by pointing out that *she* had been able to succeed only because other people were willing to delegate responsibilities to *her*. If they hadn't, she'd still be on the reception desk. Framing it this way, and showing how delegation could be a nurturing behavior, helped Nancy recognize her constant swooping as a disservice. As a senior leader in the system, she needed to give others the chance to flourish and grow, to feel their way and learn from their own mistakes.

Ilsa had Nancy create a list of every task she did for a week. She then asked her to put a mark next to only those tasks that lay within her job description, and use it as a prompt to set clearer boundaries for herself. It took discipline for Nancy to say no to people who had relied on her to do tasks that weren't checked off on her list, but as simple shifts in her behavior began to get better results, Nancy found it easier to push back. She also gained perspective on her need to please.

Nancy had always viewed herself as a naturally helpful person, and she was. But now she also saw that her habit of taking on too much was rooted in her need to feel indispensable. As Ilsa says, "Nancy had to confront the fact her over-involvement had the effect of making everything about *her*. This is usually shocking to pleasers because it doesn't fit with the 'I'm such a nice person' narrative they carry around in their heads."

THE PLEASER AT HOME

As Nancy practiced greater detachment, she began to realize that her compulsion to please was also complicating her life at home. Just as she'd undermined herself by being overly responsive at work, so was she running herself ragged trying to make sure her kids felt they had the most wonderful mother in the world on every possible occasion.

Here again, guilt was partly guiding her behavior. Because her job was demanding, she felt she needed to check every box when it came to her kids. Even when her son said, "It's fine, Mom, you really don't have to be there," she feared he might later resent her missing even a run-of-the-mill soccer practice. So her basic approach was to say yes to everything and then feel terrible if work intervened and she couldn't fulfill a promise.

Many of the mothers in her kids' school did not work. Says Nancy, "They're like supermoms, putting on these amazing birthday parties with homemade treats and decorations they whipped up themselves. One of my neighbors spent a month making these gorgeous fantasy dragon outfits for her kids at Halloween. I felt like a failure when my daughter showed up in a store-bought ghost sheet."

While Nancy had never resented her own mother's low-key approach to festivities, she feared her own kids would suffer if she failed to keep pace with neighborhood expectations. And she didn't want her family—or, to be honest, the other mothers at school—to think she was a big shot with more important things to do.

The sociologist Juliet Schor notes that contemporary culture has evolved what she calls "the most labor-intensive style of mothering the world has ever seen," a level of involvement in children's lives that is without precedent. What's baffling and ironic is that this has occurred *at precisely the same time* that women have entered the workplace in significant numbers and begun to achieve high positions.

In earlier generations, when far fewer women were employed, parents were rarely expected to show up at their kids' sports practices or ferry them to a heavy schedule of after-school events. Kids rode bikes around the neighborhood or played in the woods or basement. Birthday parties were mostly about ice cream and cake. Schor notes the deep conflict this shift sets up for women, whose guilt about working can make them reluctant to push back against expectations they realize are over-the-top.

Social media only intensifies the pressure as documenting events becomes as important as the events themselves. As one skeptical mother notes, "Someone will post photos from their kid's party on Facebook. Say the party has a circus theme. The cake is in the shape of a circus wagon and all the kids are given circus costumes to wear. Maybe it gets widely shared. All of a sudden, the other mothers feel like they need to come up with something adorable and original."

The result? "Everyone keeps ratcheting things up, and the working moms either feel like failures because they can't keep up or end up spending insane amounts of money on a six-year-old's party. At a certain point, the kids become almost secondary—it's all about the photos. Certainly the husbands couldn't care less. Sometimes I want to yell out to everyone: *Can we please just agree to stop?*"

The only way off this accelerated treadmill is to be clear about your priorities and have the confidence to stand your ground and push back against expectations that have little to do with what really matters to you or, in many cases, your children. Otherwise the demands, being endless, will consume you.

Nancy says, "Once I got comfortable accepting that my primary purpose in life wasn't pleasing everyone else, I realized I needed to make time for what was important to me and my family as opposed to what other people seemed to value. For example, I've always disliked crafts, so there's no point in spending time on that because it's what a great mom is supposed to do or because Instagram is full of cute pictures of moms and their daughters making wreaths."

Nancy began having more honest conversations at home. She says, "I had to get real and give my family a sense of my schedule and commitments. If I couldn't do something, everyone needed to know. Being honest, treating my family like partners, made a huge difference in how we communicate. We're much more relaxed together now."

Coaches who work with women report that the disease to please is becoming more problematic because expectations are constantly ratcheting up. This is an unspoken elephant in the room at many of the women's conferences we attend, where programs on "achieving balance" have become a standard part of the repertoire.

On one hand, women are urged to "go for it" and aspire to leadership at the highest level. On the other, they're warned about the consequences of missing virtually any activity involving their kids. The fact that balance is now more often described as "work-life integration" doesn't change the basic message, which is that women not only can "have it all," but that they are fatally flawed if they do not.

To retain any serenity in this ramped-up environment, you need to think long and carefully about your priorities. Not what would please others, not what would make everyone think you're the most wonderful person they've ever worked with or met, but what you in your heart want to be and achieve in your life. Given all the distractions and pressures you face, and the multiplicity of paths to feeling guilty, finding a way to push back against the disease to please is more essential than ever.

CHAPTER 13

Habit 9: Minimizing

A few years ago, Sally attended the meeting of a national women's organization that was holding its annual conference in New Orleans. After keynoting the big event, she was asked to sit in with the board to offer some thoughts on the group's new strategic plan.

The meeting took place in a glass-walled conference room atop a downtown hotel. The board was large; more than thirty people were expected. Most held high-profile corporate, academic, or nonprofit positions. About a third of the board members were men.

The room was cramped, so seating was crowded and haphazard. Flight delays caused by storms meant a fair number of people trickled in late. But as Sally tried to focus on the details of the plan being presented, she was primarily struck by the contrasting ways male and female board members responded to late arrivals.

Virtually every woman acknowledged newcomers by signaling that there was sufficient room for them to get comfortable. They pointed out empty seats, scooted their chairs aside to create more space, or found new seats for themselves at the room's periphery. They also made themselves physically smaller, pressing their legs together, holding their arms against their sides, shoving their purses under the table, even positioning their notepads more squarely in front of them.

The men reacted differently. They nodded acknowledgment— or not—but made no attempt to take up less space. Those who were spread out or had an arm flung across an empty chair remained in position. Those whose belongings were scattered about did not move them. They stayed as they were, trusting the newcomers, all accomplished adults, to figure out their own seating accommodations.

Fascinated by the dynamic, Sally began noticing body language in other situations and found it similar to what she had seen in New Orleans. In general, women acknowledged others by minimizing the space they took up, even if it caused disruption. Men did not.

Now, it's easy to interpret the women's gestures as welcoming, inclusive, generous, a measure of how attuned they are to other people and their needs. And in fact, all of this is true. And there's certainly nothing admirable about men sprawling all over the place, taking up multiple chairs and spreading their belongings about. Being clueless about the needs and physical comfort of others is not a behavior you want to adapt if you're seeking to move to the next level. But trying to shrink yourself isn't a great idea either.

SMALL

If you're in the habit of acknowledging the existence of others by trying to make yourself smaller or taking a seat at the back of the room, you might want to consider how well this response serves you. As research conducted by social scientists and neuroscientists confirms—and many of us know from experience—when you draw in your arms and legs, tighten your body, hunker down, or move aside—you undermine your ability to project authority and power.

Not only do others read you as diminished, you begin to feel that way yourself. That's because your physical attempts to shrink send a message to your brain that you really shouldn't be occupying your space, either physically or metaphorically. *You're not big enough, so you don't belong. Others are more deserving than you are.* That's how your brain interprets your actions.

It's hardly surprising that your body would send such a signal, since trying to get small is a classic submissive behavior. You've probably observed your dog lower his eyes and flip down his tail when a more dominant dog approaches. Or you've watched your cat slick back her ears and flatten her fur as she slinks past the dog. The message your pets are sending is clear: *I'm really tiny. I pose no threat. Take no notice. Just allow me to get out of your way.*

However unintended, or well intended—for example, the desire to welcome a newcomer—when you try to make yourself smaller, you send a subservient message to everyone in the room. This happens without your consciously meaning to do so. It happens simply because you're a mammal.

Being a human mammal, of course, means that you also have the ability to use speech to minimize your presence. This is another habit that serves to diminish your power. Fortunately, there's been enough attention paid in recent years to the female practice of routinely apologizing that you may have become vigilant in avoiding it. When you hear "I'm sorry" falling too easily from your lips, or when you use the phrase pointlessly to open a conversation ("I'm sorry, I need to ask..."), you may have learned to catch yourself and self-correct.

Yet other language minimizers persist, such as (in English) the constant use of the word *just*. As in: "I just need a minute of your time." "I just want to say something." "I just have one observation." The word *only* can serve the same purpose. Other minimizers include *little, tiny, small,* and *quick,* used to suggest that you won't be taking up the other person's valuable time with something you nevertheless believe is important enough to mention: "I only have one tiny suggestion." Or, "If I could make a very minor point."

Even more egregious, but unfortunately common, are verbal discounters and disclaimers. "Maybe this isn't important." "You may already have thought of this." "This may be beside the point." These verbal tics are usually employed at the start of a statement, where they are calculated to do the most harm. The millennial habit of routinely ending every sentence on a rising note, which has the effect of making every statement sound like a question, conveys an uncertainty that both minimizes and discounts, while also seeming designed to invite contradiction.

In addition to implicitly saying, "Please don't mind me," minimizers and discounters convey uncertainty. They are yet another tool you can use to undermine your power. A study done at the Harvard Business School, "Who Gets Heard and Why," found that women are more likely than men to downplay their certainty when they speak, hedging assertions and proactively acknowledging that others may hold different points of view.

It's not surprising that many women have adopted these habits, since certainty is often interpreted as arrogance, and women tend to fear getting tagged as arrogant. There's good reason for this, of course, since women who are perceived as arrogant tend to be viewed in highly negative terms, whereas arrogance in men is often interpreted as confidence and boldness.

Nevertheless, as the Harvard study confirms, conveying uncertainty is a good way to assure you will not be heard. People in positions of power tend to read uncertainty as a lack of commitment or preparedness. Given the no-win nature of the dilemma—you're either seen as arrogant or lacking in commitment—it's usually a good practice to just come out and say what you mean.

SOFT

Minimizing behaviors and figures of speech are particularly challenging for women raised in cultures that place a high value on female modesty and self-effacement. Aiko, an engineer Marshall worked with in Japan, had been taught as a child that women should be tentative, hesitant, and very quiet, keeping their voices soft and even walking with minimal sound. Speaking up and being direct were viewed as coarse, rude, and "noisy," evidence of a poor upbringing that reflected badly on a woman's entire family. When she stood her ground or tried to speak with authority, Aiko felt she was dishonoring those she loved.

Humility, deference, and minimizing are in fact hallmarks of the distinctive "women's language" that well-brought-up women in Japan were until recently expected to use throughout their lives. It's a legacy that can get in the way as women in this culture seek to move to higher levels, where they are expected to speak as equals with powerful men.

Abandoning habits of deference can also be difficult for women from cultures where they have been taught to avoid making eye contact with men, to refrain from shaking hands, and to speak only when directly addressed. Such expectations and traditions make it difficult for women to project ease in mixed settings, which can hold them back from reaching their full potential.

Many cultures also view indirectness as a polite behavior for women. Even cultures that pride themselves on being direct often subtly encourage women to diminish their impact by presenting an idea obliquely. This can take the form of prefacing an assertion with unnecessary explanation: "First, let me tell you how I came up with this idea." As you'll see in the following chapter, such preliminary hedging is often heard as offering too much information. Given that, it's usually most effective to be direct.

WE

As noted in Chapter 5, if you struggle to claim your achievements, you may habitually use *we* instead of *I.* Even when describing an accomplishment that's primarily or entirely your own, you may frame it as *we* because you want to seem polite and inclusive. This may sometimes be appropriate, but often it merely serves to minimize what you contribute.

In addition to underplaying your achievements, habitually speaking in the *we* voice can sow confusion about your role in a specific effort. Did you lead it? Were you essential to the outcome? Or was somebody else the hero? What exactly is "we" intended to convey?

Psychologist James Pennebaker, writing in the *Harvard Busi-*

ness Review, notes that a cross-cultural study of pronoun use reveals that women actually use the *I* word more than men. This is not surprising, since women tend to talk more, use more words when they talk (see the following chapter), and speak more freely about their intimate feelings. In fact, Pennebaker attributes women's use of *I* to their attunement with their inner state and comfort with personal conversation, in contrast to men, who are more likely to speak about objects and events. But this is true for communication in general, as opposed to in the workplace. In professional situations, women who are otherwise comfortable with self-disclosure routinely resort to *we* when speaking of their own success—as Amy the non-profit leader did in Chapter 5.

It's not difficult to guess why this would be so, since speaking about your accomplishments is an inherently assertive behavior and women are often penalized for seeming assertive. As Sheryl Sandberg and Adam Grant, writing in the *New York Times*, have shown, women who speak assertively are far more likely than men to be viewed negatively at work—a finding your own experience may confirm. Yet as Sandberg and Grant also found, women who *fail* to assert themselves also tend to be viewed in negative terms. The real problem, they conclude, "seems to be speaking while female."

One way to finesse this double bind when it comes to talking about your achievements is to give your team or co-workers credit for a joint success while also articulating how you supported or strengthened the team's efforts. This has the effect of turning a lose-lose scenario into a win for you and a win for your colleagues. Splitting the difference can make everyone happy.

And especially if you're speaking with a confident male leader who has no problem claiming credit, constantly referring to *we* may suggest to him that you had nothing to do with a successful effort. So given the choice between sounding self-centered and underplaying your hard-earned achievements, you're probably better off forthrightly using *I*.

HOLD YOUR SPACE

Whenever you use words or actions that minimize your presence or contribution, you show uncertainty about your right to take up space—to hold it, to occupy it, to inhabit it fully. Others tend to read this hesitancy as a failure to really show up and the inability to project a strong and engaged presence.

For decades, Sally has been asked what women can do to convey a more powerful leadership presence. Questions tend to focus on the cosmetics: the right clothes, a firm handshake, a confident tone of voice, whether a woman should carry a purse, even whether plastic surgery can be helpful(!).

Yet decades of exposure to a wide range of extraordinary leaders have shown both of us that *the* key component of leadership presence is the opposite of cosmetic: it lies in the capacity to be fully present. Present for a task, for a conversation, for the moment, for an opportunity. Present for your larger purpose in the world.

As it turns out, there's a reason the words *presence* and *present* are related.

Today's high-intensity, technology-saturated, 24-7 work environment makes it difficult for anyone to be present, but women face particular challenges. Multiple responsibilities can scatter your attention. Home as well as work requires professional skills, which can make every day feel like a marathon you just need to get *through*. And women's capacity for broad-spectrum notice—the radar that will be described in Chapter 16—is a great potential strength that nevertheless comes with a downside: it can make it tough to focus.

Yet even as the capacity to be present grows more challenging, the benefits of doing so increase. This becomes truer as you move to a higher level.

For example, being present is the most powerful way to connect across cultures, which makes it valuable for leaders in a diverse global environment. People from very different cultures can immediately read whether you are fully available to them, because your body language always lets them know. Think about it. You can't calm a small child if you're checking your cell phone. You can't train a dog or a horse if you're worrying about what your boss said this morning. And if a three-year-old and a member of a different species can tell whether you're engaged, a fellow adult from a different cultural background surely can.

In addition, empathy, which is increasingly recognized as an essential leadership skill, depends on your ability to be present for another person. Research demonstrates that you feel empathy when you are attending to another person so closely that your neural pathways start mirroring one another's. Empathic behavior therefore depends on your capacity to show up fully. When you're distracted, you can neither feel nor project empathy.

New research cited by Susan David in her recent book *Emotional Agility* demonstrates another benefit of presence for women. She notes that, although women often struggle to be heard, they in fact receive *as much attention* as men when speaking in public if (and only if) they are perceived as being fully present. Being present also has the effect of making women seem more credible and authoritative. This powerful finding adds to the evidence that the ability to rest in the moment and hold your space is vital for women seeking to project leadership presence.

The capacity to be present requires freeing your attention so you can show up where you are. And because of the special challenges as well as the specific benefits described above, the ability to do so can be especially valuable for women.

So what can you do to free your attention so you can fully inhabit where you are? You might start by pushing back against compulsive multitasking, a practice women often seem to take perverse pride in. Swearing it off entirely is impractical, but it's important to realize that, while multitasking feels efficient, it always comes with a cost. For the fact is that doing two things at once makes it impossible to be present for either because your attention is by definition fragmented. And fragmented attention is a highly effective minimizer.

Multitasking is also the quickest route to mental exhaustion, the true source of which is not being busy but the strain you put on your brain when you do two things at once. By contrast, research into meditation and other mindfulness practices shows that the most powerful way to reenergize and refresh yourself is by focusing your attention on one thing instead of permitting it to bounce all over.

Multitasking also diminishes you by giving the impression that you're overly responsive to random events. If you see someone constantly checking her phone in a meeting, you don't think, *Wow, she must be important.* And you certainly don't think, *What a strong presence she exudes.* Instead, you're likely to conclude that she isn't in control of her own time or schedule and is therefore incapable of showing up for what's actually going on. By demonstrating over-responsiveness, she minimizes both her importance and her presence.

The good news is that permitting your attention to be fragmented is not a character flaw. It's just a habit, like minimizing, hedging, softening, shrinking, and ceding space. These behaviors don't necessarily betray deep-seated insecurities. They're just ways of responding you've grown accustomed to over the years, reflexes you may already have outgrown. They may have helped you at some point, but they will undermine you as you reach higher by making it impossible for you to manifest—or enjoy—serenity and power.

CHAPTER 14

Habit 10: Too Much

As a woman, you may have found yourself having to tamp down your emotional register when you're in professional situations, especially around high-performing men. You may do this in an effort to match your mood to the prevailing workplace and leadership culture. Or because you've gotten feedback that you come on too strong or are too intense.

Women frequently hear these comments, but knowing how to address them can be confusing. On the one hand, there are definite costs to being tagged as being "a bit too much," particularly as you move higher. You may be seen as unprofessional or unreliable when you are neither of these things. You may get called out for not being "a good fit."

On the other hand, having to constantly repress your natural responses can make you feel awkward, inauthentic, and stiff, draining away the zest and enthusiasm you need to perform at the highest level. Excessive self-monitoring can depress your energy and inhibit your ability to be your best self. It can kill spontaneity and so undermine your ability to have an impact.

Routinely repressing your feelings can also diminish your

capacity to inspire trust. Co-workers may interpret your reluctance to respond from the heart as evidence that you're hiding something. They may wonder what's up with you, why you can't just be real. Most likely they're blissfully unaware of how criticism you've received in the past makes you hesitate to be direct.

The too much/not enough divide is another of those "damned if you do, damned if you don't" double binds that frequently plague women, and become more problematic as you move to a higher level. The pain of dealing with this conundrum, and the difficulty of locating that sweet spot between letting it all hang out and keeping yourself tightly under wraps, adds an extra burden that can make you feel as if you don't belong.

If you work in a mostly male environment, the negative effects of expressing your feelings can be compounded by the difficulty men often have responding to women. Some men resent women's ability to be vulnerable. They've had to repress displays of hurt and fear all their lives, so why should women be allowed to show their feelings? It seems unfair, a form of female privilege. Other men feel manipulated by any expression of strong female emotion because they believe they have to "do something" to assuage or contain it. If they don't know what to do, they may feel resentful. The upshot is that the whole business of emotional expression can be a landmine for women.

Women's emotional range is of course not limited to expressing vulnerability. You may also get feedback that you are "too enthusiastic" because you greet new ideas and suggestions with immediate and wholehearted endorsement. In many cases, a simple desire to support and encourage others lies at the root of this response. But in a buttoned-up culture, it gets misinterpreted.

We've seen women falter on both sides of the too much/not

enough divide. But we've also watched women resolve the conflict to their advantage. Recognizing that success in any endeavor requires discipline, they find a way to bring their immediate reactions to full awareness and then respond with passion tempered by experience and intention. As this way of responding becomes a habit, they take on an emotional gravitas that draws integrity from the intensity of the effort.

The usual culprits in the "too much" scenario for women are too much emotion, too many words, and too much disclosure. And while the path to addressing these critiques is similar, each calls for different specifics.

TOO MUCH EMOTION

In his work with male clients, Marshall finds that anger is the emotion most likely to get in their way. As he notes in the original *What Got You Here*, successful men who lash out in anger often justify doing so as a "useful management tool." They imagine it's an effective way to motivate sluggish employees and send a strong message about the importance of whatever is at stake. Yet the routine use of anger actually has the opposite effect, causing people to shut down, tune out, and lose motivation.

Of course, both women and men react in anger at work. But in our experience, women are more likely to display strong emotion in the form of anxiety, resentment, frustration, or fear. And the expression of these painful sensations is the primary reason many women get tagged as being volatile or "too emotional."

Men of course also experience these emotions. But they've usually grown accustomed to stuffing them, or to channeling fear and anxiety into aggression. The message that anger is the only acceptable way for men to display emotion is conveyed from early childhood and finds reinforcement in team sports, where anger may be viewed as a sign of competitive drive.

Parents and teachers (as well as coaches) tend to give girls more latitude in displaying hurt, fear, and frustration or otherwise letting their vulnerability show. So it's not surprising that women tend to be more comfortable acting on these emotions. But given that the leadership model in most organizations has been set in the male image, these emotions find little acceptance, even though they're usually less destructive than anger.

Let's be clear. What you *feel* is not the problem. There's no such thing as a good or bad emotion. Your emotions have enormous value. They provide useful information about the situation you're in, vital clues you would be unwise to ignore. Emotions are the wellspring of your intuition and the prime source of your energy and passion. They get you out of bed in the morning and keep you engaged when the going gets rough.

So it's vitally important to recognize what you are feeling at any moment, to identify and accept the emotions your circumstances are stirring up. However, *speaking* while in the grip of strong emotion is usually a bad practice. Your perceptions about who's at fault may be distorted. You may overstate your case. You may come across as touchy or out of control. And you most certainly will be unable to calibrate your response in a way that lands with maximum impact.

To recap: Feeling and identifying your emotion gives you power. Reacting to what you feel squanders it.

Rosa, a native of Colombia, is an executive in a construction firm with projects all over the Amazon basin. She's also the client of one of our coaching colleagues. It's rare to find a woman in her position in her part of the world and her sector, but Rosa attributes a good part of her success to her ability to harness her strong emotions and make them work in her favor.

Learning to do this was not easy. Early in her career, Rosa was often stereotyped as a volcanic Latina; it didn't help that she looked like Sofia Vergara. But being called "too emotional" once too often made Rosa determined to find a way to temper and use her emotion instead of letting it get in her way.

She describes a typical situation. "I was in a meeting recently in São Paulo. We'd just met with some investment partners and things had not gone well. Our executive team was venting about what they'd heard and doubting the good faith of our partners. But the primary emotion I kept hearing from them was desperation. As in, *no matter what, we've got to make this thing work.*"

As the only woman in the room, Rosa knew she couldn't afford to get worked up. So she did what she always tries to do. "I waited patiently, listened to what everyone was saying, and tried to tap into what *I* was feeling. I realized my dominant emotion was actually dread. And that while part of me wanted to go through with the deal, which we'd been working on for over a year, I knew in my heart that it would be a mistake."

When she was clear about what she was feeling and sensed a lull in the conversation, Rosa spoke, keeping her voice firm and low. Here's her account of what she said:

"I feel obligated to be very honest with you as my colleagues. I'm uncomfortable with the direction this project is taking and sense many of you feel this way as well. You all know I have a good record of being right when I listen to my gut, and I am listening to it now. This deal still looks great on paper so I understand its appeal. But I fear we haven't thought through the implications of partnering with this firm. I believe our partnership with them could tarnish our reputation and bring public scrutiny that could weigh us down for years. So I recommend we slow things down and do more research. I'm glad to work with anyone who wants to join me in this effort. I know this is not what you want to hear, but I need to honor my very strong sense of what our next step should be."

Rosa's way of responding was powerful: confident, measured, and authentic, explicitly rooted in emotion yet expressed in terms that appeal to logic and common sense. She did not repress the fear she was feeling but adopted a modulated rather than fearful tone that gave her colleagues permission to take a breath and get off the emotion train.

Rosa's offer to work with a few of the men present to get more information was also highly intentional. It assured that she'd have allies should their findings confirm that her company needed to walk away from the project. This took her out of the business of being the lone Cassandra warning of potential disaster—a thankless role that women who are in touch with their intuitive responses often assume.

It's important to notice how completely authentic Rosa was being, how accurately she described her fear, and how firmly she spoke her truth. As a woman who had in the past been criticized for being "too emotional," Rosa knew her power lay in acknowledging the precise nature of her emotion while maintaining an authoritative tone, grounded in passion but guided by perspective.

TOO MANY WORDS

Research shows that women speak an average of 20,000 words a day while men typically speak around 7,000. So it's not surprising that women operating in male-centric cultures that privilege succinctness often receive feedback that they're too talkative or offer "TMI."

Typical objections include taking too much time to get to the point, prefacing a suggestion with a lot of background, speaking in sentences instead of bullets, obscuring the main topic with side observations, overexplaining, offering multiple rationales and examples, chatting during awkward pauses, and volunteering explanations instead of waiting to be asked.

Such wordiness can be caused by insecurity, but it is often simply a counterproductive habit rooted in behaviors that may reflect your greatest strengths. These include a gift for establishing intimacy and forging strong relationships, a genuine care for and interest in others, and the capacity to notice important details that others overlook. The challenge in becoming a more effective communicator is to retain these strengths while addressing the habits that undermine you.

In her programs, Sally often works with women on becoming more concise. Recently, she received some powerful reinforcement. She was delivering a daylong workshop in Singapore with a group of high-potential women at a global biotech company and moderating a panel of senior leaders. Sally asked Sherry, a panelist who headed worldwide diabetes research for the company, what she believed had been the quality most responsible for her success.

Without hesitation, Sherry cited her ability to be concise.

She explained that she'd developed this skill during her medical career prior to joining the company. She said, "Doing rounds as a resident and then being in private practice for twenty years forced me to be succinct, even though I'm from the American South and have the typical gift of gab. But when you're in practice, you have an extremely short time with patients and a lot of important information to deliver. So you learn to focus on what is most essential. If you start to elaborate or go into detail, you'll run out of time and shortchange the next person. Plus you may overwhelm your patients with too many facts."

Sherry's efforts proved great preparation for the corporate world, where attention spans can be punishingly short and a "get to the bottom line" mentality prevails, especially at senior levels. She noted, "After meetings, male executives would comment on how quickly I'd gotten to the point. It was as if I'd performed some kind of miracle!" Sherry then began noticing how impatient many of these same senior leaders were with women who were less concise.

She said, "The women in our company are great, but a lot of them overcommunicate. There's a definite male tone in meetings here, an expectation that people will be very crisp and never say anything superfluous. It's seen as being professional and authoritative. Women often like to start with a backstory—'let me tell you how I came up with this idea'—and offer a lot of detail. This is how they talk to each another, which is fine. But the men here, especially at the executive level, tend to lose interest when there's a lot of elaboration. And when they lose interest, they lose interest *fast.*"

Sherry notes that being concise takes preparation. "You need to pare everything down to the minimum, which means thinking through in advance what matters most. If that's not your natural speaking style, if you tend to be more expansive, that's going to require some work, even rehearsal. But with practice, it's a skill women can easily learn."

Sherry now does a fair amount of internal coaching to help women in her company be more succinct. Before a meeting, she may arrange to send a subtle signal if she notices a female colleague going on too long. "It really helps to let women know in real time when they're not being as effective as they could be. They accept it from me because they know I'm on their side and because they want to have more impact. Now I see women signaling one another when they hear phrases like, 'let me give you a little background.' That kind of support is really making a difference."

TOO MUCH DISCLOSURE

Disclosure presents another "too much" behavior that can bedevil women in the workplace, undermining their capacity to be seen as trusted and discreet professionals who carry themselves as leaders. In our experience, women who overdisclose usually do so for one of two reasons. Either they assume that building good relationships and finding common ground requires the sharing of personal information, or they're convinced that being authentic depends on disclosure.

Let's look at each of these beliefs in turn.

It's not difficult to understand why women might assume that the building of strong relationships is sustained by self-disclosure. Researchers like Deborah Tannen who study women's communication styles note that women deploy personal information as the primary means of bonding with one another. They share private hopes and dreams but also dissect their faults and problems, detail doubts about themselves, and reveal the messy details of troubled relationships. This frank exchange of shared vulnerabilities creates a feeling of intimacy and is regarded as a sign of trust.

By contrast, men rarely build relationships by exchanging intimacies or dissecting problems. Men are in fact most likely to bond with one another by doing things together, often in highly competitive situations. So a subtle (or not so subtle) one-upmanship often characterizes male bonding. This dynamic leaves no place for the sharing of vulnerabilities.

The difference in male and female bonding styles generally serves women well, making them more likely than men to form close and long-lasting friendships. Many researchers believe that women's zest for building intimate personal friendships and resilient support networks is one reason women live longer than men and report being happier in virtually every culture, except those in which their autonomy is severely restricted.

But workplace cultural standards around the world have been almost entirely set by men, especially at the leadership level. Trust at work is generally viewed as a matter of competence and reliability rather than frank exchanges about what makes you tick. This is why routine personal disclosure, especially the sharing of doubts and weaknesses—"I guess I'm insecure" or "sometimes I feel lonely in this job"—is more likely to diminish your credibility than to win you a place in your co-workers' hearts. Although the emotional tenor of the workplace is shifting as women gain greater influence and personal information is more freely exchanged than in the past, disclosure still represents a landmine for many women.

The habit of disclosure can also be rooted in the simple belief that talking about your problems and weaknesses is the most direct route to being, and being viewed as, authentic.

Authenticity has become a workplace buzzword in recent years, with much talk about the importance of bringing your "real self" to work. The idea is that being fully yourself will free you to be more creative, connect more deeply with colleagues, and find a more passionate point of engagement with your work.

Certainly there's a degree of truth in this, and pretending you're someone you're not is never going to qualify as a good practice. But the relentless emphasis on authenticity can be a trap, blurring boundaries that most organizations continue to honor and enforce even as they sing the praises of authentic engagement. And it's a trap most likely to ensnare women, who may feel encouraged to abandon qualities of professionalism and discretion in the pursuit of being fully authentic.

CHAPTER 15

Habit 11: Ruminating

Ruminating is a variation on Clinging to the Past, which was Habit 13 in Marshall's original book. If you cling to the past, you probably spend a lot of time reliving unfortunate things that happened. You put energy into trying to rewrite events instead of accepting them and moving on. You mull, you dwell, you re-litigate, you regret. You tell yourself that you're figuring things out in order to understand exactly what went wrong. But at a certain point, reviewing what went wrong at some moment in the past begins to undermine you, and hinder your ability to rise.

Both men and women derail themselves by focusing on the past. But they often do so in different ways. In Marshall's experience, men who cling to the past tend to blame others for what they believe has gone wrong in their own lives or careers, making excuses for themselves and turning their regret outward. The result is anger. This is not surprising, as anger is the emotion men are usually most comfortable feeling, as research confirms, and as we noted in the previous chapter.

Women, by contrast, are more likely to turn regret inward, blaming themselves and dissecting their own mistakes. You may stress over minor faux pas and micro-misunderstandings in which you perceive yourself to have been at fault. Or you may agonize over miscalculations that really did set you back but are long over-due for being let go.

Routinely mulling over your mistakes, regrets, and negative experiences is called rumination. It's a habit of mind that psychol-ogists tell us is more often found in women than in men. That's because women not only spend more time reliving their setbacks, they are more likely to believe that whatever went wrong was all their fault.

It's a habit that does not serve women well.

The word *rumination* offers a clue to what's involved. Techni-cally, rumination describes what ruminants do. Ruminants are animals such as cows, goats, sheep, and deer that live exclusively on plant food and so struggle to extract sufficient protein from their diet. To solve the problem, evolution has provided rumi-nants with a special stomach that predigests their food. The food then travels back up into their mouths, where it is broken down by further chewing before moving into a second stomach to be digested. This process is popularly known as "chewing the cud." And while it's a brilliant evolutionary strategy for ruminants, it does little for human beings.

If you spend time ruminating, you may tell yourself that you're being reflective. You may imagine it will help you avoid mistakes in the future. Or you may subconsciously believe that you *deserve* to feel terrible because your behavior fell short of an imagined ideal or sent a signal you did not intend.

But in fact, there's little protein to be extracted from the well-chewed morsels of self-contempt that you as a human ruminant keep coming up with. What you're actually doing when you ruminate is berating yourself, engaging in a kind of self-talk that can border on abuse.

In his coaching practice, Marshall has seen women at the pinnacle of success who nevertheless constantly go back over their mistakes and take responsibility for events over which they in fact had little control. He finds that the energy these women waste in feeling bad about themselves diminishes their ability to be effective and reap the benefits of their otherwise superb leadership skills.

While men practice plenty of self-defeating behaviors, Marshall rarely finds men getting bogged down in self-castigation. Men are more likely to say, "I made a mistake. We all do. It is time to move on."

FEELING WORSE AND BEING STUCK

Rumination is counterproductive for two reasons. First, it always makes you feel worse. And second, it gets in the way of your ability to resolve your problems.

You feel worse because the more you chew over past events, the more your brain gets accustomed to chewing. As the neural grooves of self-blame and regret get established, rumination becomes your default mode. So when anything goes wrong—which, this being life on earth, frequently happens—you immediately start rerunning your default mental tapes. *Why did I say that? What must she have thought? When will I stop being such a jerk? Will I never learn? What the hell is wrong with me?*

These self-accusatory scripts are perfectly calculated to depress you. And in fact, psychologists draw a straight line of causation between chronic rumination and chronic depression. Dwelling on the negative and berating yourself is bad for your health, physical and mental. And the longer your mind is consumed with gloomy self-accusations, the worse you will feel.

Rumination also inhibits taking action to remedy what got you ruminating in the first place. Researchers note that ruminators often continue analyzing their situation even *after* they've developed a plan for dealing with it. In fact, ruminators spend so much time mulling things over that many never get around to coming up with a solution. They're more comfortable remaining stuck in the problem.

Nevertheless, the sheer act of mulling can make you feel as if you're being productive. This gives you a nice excuse for continuing to mull. You tell yourself that fully dissecting your situation will enable you to do things differently in the future. But the fact is, the more you ruminate, the longer you put off changing the behaviors that are causing you pain.

Susan Nolen-Hoeksema, who until her early death was the leading researcher on rumination, believed women were predisposed to it because of the high value they place on relationships. While their attentiveness to others can be a source of strength, it can also lead women to devote inordinate time to processing the often-ambiguous content of simple exchanges and scouring chance observations for potential meanings. *Why would he say that? Was it something I did? Could he have misinterpreted what I meant? Does this mean he doesn't trust me, or doesn't like me?*

"Analysis equals paralysis" is a slogan made for ruminants. So it's not surprising that the phrase is used a lot in twelve-step recovery programs, or that chronic rumination is considered a risk factor for substance abuse. You create a hell in your mind and then try to escape it using excessive food or alcohol or an excessive behavior. But it's always waiting for you when you're done with your bender. In this way, rumination functions like an addiction.

BREAKING FREE

Dr. Nolen-Hoeksema's researches led her to believe that interruption and distraction were the most effective means of putting a brake on rumination. An unexpected encounter or targeted moment of feedback is often just what's needed to shake the ruminator free from her self-imposed torpor.

Such an encounter helped break the cycle for Liza, a film producer Sally worked with. Liza had enjoyed early success as a production manager for a small but highly profitable film company, where she quickly developed a warm relationship with her CEO. Joe valued Liza's skill at keeping costs low and bringing in projects on time, while somehow never alienating talent with her demands. After a few years, Joe made sure Liza reported directly to him. She came to view him as family.

But an influx of capital from a new investor seemed to fire Joe's ambitions. He hired a new producer to handle a few big-budget deals. Mike was younger than Liza but had major studio experience. Though his jobs had been relatively junior, he was a big talker with even bigger ideas. Joe seemed dazzled by his young hotshot, and took Mike under his wing, green-lighting even half-thought-through projects that burned up cash. Liza's projects continued to get funding but were increasingly viewed as marginal: low-budget cash cows that could sustain the company's more high-profile brand.

It drove Liza crazy. "I went from being Joe's favorite to being a nobody in the company. I used to go to the film festivals and parties with Joe but now he invited Mike. Mike was like Joe's son while I was the slightly embarrassing stepdaughter. I was totally consumed with trying to figure out what I'd done wrong. Had Joe always disliked my films? Did he think I wasn't Hollywood enough? Should I dress up more when I came to the office? Should I be nicer to his new wife? Or did he hate me because I'd been so friendly with his old one?"

As Liza stewed and grew ever more miserable, she began retreating into her shell. She felt isolated, rejected, and very much alone. It was a chance meeting with Joe's former wife at a café after a particularly discouraging day at work that finally jolted Liza from what was fast becoming a downward spiral of rumination.

She says, "Ida and I were so happy to see each other. I hadn't realized how much I'd missed her. We started talking, and after a while I poured my heart out about all that had happened with Joe and Mike. She listened for a long time and then she stopped me. She said, 'Liza, I keep hearing you try to figure out what you did wrong, but you've got to realize this is so not about you. This is about Joe and his desire to change everything about his life—his family, where he lives, his company, who he is in the industry, who he hangs out with. Please stop trying to figure out what happened or how it could have been different. Start thinking about what *you* are going to do. That's what I did—and I was his wife. It should be easier for you.'"

The conversation had a big effect on Liza. To begin with, it forced her to revise her self-blaming script. Once she accepted that Joe's crisis had nothing to do with her, she saw the futility of going over it endlessly in her mind. As her self-accusatory mood lifted, she was able to focus on her own future. Clearly, she had a choice to make. She could accept that there were many things she still loved about her job and make peace with that. Or she could take her skills to a new company where she might be more appreciated.

After a few months, Liza decided to leave her job. She says, "It was agony because I'd grown up in the company, but by the time I was ready to resign, I mostly felt grateful for the opportunities I'd been given. Joe had done a lot for me, but now it was time to start looking forward. If Ida had, I could too."

MEN MOVE ON

Of course, it's better to stop rumination in its tracks before the habit gets established, pushing back whenever a negative script works its way into your thoughts. Gina, the chief marketing executive at a media company and former coaching client of Julie Johnson, found a simple way to do this. Julie learned about it during a catch-up lunch when she asked Gina what had been most helpful about their collaboration.

Gina said, "By far the most important thing was when you said to me, *men move on*. They might have their faults, but they don't usually worry all that much about them. And now I sit in these executive meetings with a lot of crosscurrents and power plays going on, and my mind is doing its best to get onto its old familiar track. Maybe I'm wondering, *Does Peter think my idea is stupid? Was I a jerk for bringing it up? And do I really belong in the room with these hotshot guys?* In other words, I'm heading down the rab-bit hole, telling myself I'm not good enough, but then I manage to pull myself back. I do it by reminding myself that *men move on.* What I mean is, *Men move on, so I can move on too.* I don't have to get caught up with these negative thoughts. I can find a way to let them go."

Julie says, "I loved when Gina told me that. Because in my experience, rumination is a real killer for women. It keeps even brilliant and talented women stuck. Plus it can destroy you at the executive level, where you need to seem, and *be*, confident and decisive. And because at that level, you're around men who really know how to move on."

So if you identify as a ruminant, please write a new script for yourself. And repeat firmly after us: *rumination is for cows!*

CHAPTER 16

Habit 12: Letting Your Radar Distract You

O ne of women's great strengths is their capacity for broad-spectrum notice, the ability to notice a lot of things at once. In researching *The Female Vision*, Sally and Julie Johnson found that neuroscientists have documented this capacity using functional MRIs, which give a picture of the brain in operation. These scans show that when women process information, their brains light up in a lot of different regions, taking in a multiplicity of details. By contrast, when men process information, their brain activity tends to be concentrated in one region.

The result? Women's attention for the most part operates like radar, scanning the environment, picking up a broad range of clues, and paying attention to context. Whereas men's attention operates more like a laser, focusing tightly and absorbing information in sequence.

Of course, all human beings fall at different places along this spectrum. Some women have a more laser-like noticing style and some men have more well-developed radar. Noticing styles also change over time, depending on how they are used. Because human neural circuits adapt, grow and shrink as you practice different behaviors, your brain develops new abilities depending on which circuits get used. So if your job requires you to analyze a lot of data, your neural paths will become more laser-like over time. If your job requires you to be aware of people's responses, the neural paths that support radar will become more robust.

Still, the generalization about men's and women's different noticing styles remains broadly true, as fMRI results confirm. This makes sense given that our distinctive ways of noticing have evolved over hundreds of thousands of years. The differences probably go back to the hunter-gatherer era, when men were responsible for spearing large animals for food, a skill that requires focus, while women gathered nuts, roots, and berries, activities that depend on broad-spectrum notice. Having primary charge of small children, a demand that has remained constant through the millennia, has no doubt contributed to women's capacity for radar-like notice.

One problem for women is that organizations still privilege laser notice—"just get to the bottom line"—and view it as a leadership behavior. This is not surprising given that, until a few decades ago, organizations were led almost entirely by men. Yet a well-developed radar can be a powerful asset at work. Being highly attuned to the details of relationships and to what people are feeling enables you to excel at motivating others, inspiring morale. It helps you negotiate and communicate with sensitivity and skill. It supports collaboration and teamwork. And radar helps you build the intimate friendships that support your resilience when the going gets rough.

THE SHADOW SIDE OF RADAR

But as with any strength, radar has its shadow side. A well-developed radar can make it difficult for you to filter out unhelpful distractions, scattering your attention and undermining your ability to be present. Radar can degrade your capacity to compartmentalize perceptions that might undermine your confidence and ability to perform.

Radar may also be in part responsible for women's tendency to give themselves a hard time. Being hyperaware of other people's reactions can feed the fires of self-doubt and cause you to overthink your actions. Having an active radar may therefore be in part responsible if you have a tendency to ruminate. Especially if you put a negative spin on whatever you notice.

Taylor is a successful executive coach whose acute radar helps her intuit what her clients need. She says, "I'm very confident one-on-one—you have to be as a coach. But I get self-conscious in larger groups because there's so much going on, so many reactions to read. This can make it hard to focus on what *I'm* trying to do."

Her radar undermined her recently when she was asked to present an overview of her practice to fifty potential corporate clients. Taylor dealt with her nervousness by thoroughly preparing and felt reasonably confident at the start of her presentation. But about ten minutes in, her concentration began to unravel.

She says, "It started when I noticed this guy in the front of the room who seemed skeptical of everything I said. He looked irritated that he even had to be there. I kept trying to figure out what was bothering him, and that got me a bit distracted. Then a woman in the back of the room started waving her hand. Even though we weren't even at the Q&A yet, I felt I had to call on her. She stood up and said my talk was not what she'd been led to expect. Apparently one of the event websites promised I'd be talking about how to structure internal coaching departments. I don't know how that happened, but it's not my area of expertise."

The woman's objection took Taylor by surprise, and she heard herself apologizing and asking what she could say that might be more helpful. "So the woman started talking about her company's coaching problems, and really yammering on. I could tell people in the room were getting restless but she just bulldozed ahead. When I was able to regain the floor, I had to race through the rest of my remarks. I felt grateful when my time was up and the next speaker took over."

At the buffet table during the break, Taylor ran into Mirette, a colleague who excels at public speaking. "I told her I thought my talk had gone badly, and she gave me a sympathetic look. Of course, that confirmed my worst suspicions."

The next morning, Taylor left Mirette a voice mail asking to schedule a quick talk. Mirette called her back immediately. "I told her I wanted an honest critique of what had gone wrong. She said she'd be glad to help. She said I'd seemed distracted even before the woman interrupted me, and asked what was going on. I told her about the guy in the front row and how I kept wondering why he seemed so negative. Since I was already struggling when the woman chimed in, I was unnerved by her disappointment and felt I had to address it."

Mirette pointed out two problems. "First, the guy in the front row. *So what* if he seemed like he didn't want to be there? Maybe he'd had a fight with his wife that morning. Maybe she told him she was filing for divorce. Maybe he was sick or hungover or mad at his boss. The point is, you had no way of knowing. But you decided it had to be about you."

Secondly, said Mirette, "You should not have tried to address the woman's disappointment. In any big crowd, there's someone like her, an irritant who tries to grab the floor and keep talking. That kind of person can only succeed if you as the speaker let them. For all you know, half of the people in the audience had heard her do it a dozen times and were waiting desperately for you to shut her down."

"You're probably right," said Taylor. "But what should I have done?"

"The best way to handle a person like that is to say you're sorry she's disappointed and then immediately and very firmly move on. Don't give her a chance to respond. You aren't there to satisfy her and, as a speaker, part of your job is to protect your audience from people who want to go off on tangents. If you don't, you're always going to lose them."

Mirette's frank assessment helped Taylor see that she'd been so busy trying to read her audience and figure out whether she was fulfilling their expectations that she'd lost sight of her presentation's content and even her purpose in giving her talk. Her sharply attuned radar, a source of success in her coaching practice, had destabilized her with a larger group.

THE LEFT-HAND COLUMN

Taylor's underlying problem was her inability to be present for her audience and what was happening in the room while also delivering her prepared presentation. This happened because, as the psychologist Chris Argyris might have put it, she allowed her left-hand column to overwhelm her right-hand column.

Argyris famously made this distinction when describing how humans allocate their attention. In your left-hand column are the random thoughts and observations that run through your brain while you're doing something else, forming your stream of consciousness. In your right-hand column is the task or conversation you're supposed to be showing up for.

It's easy to see how a highly attuned radar might overstimulate your left-hand column, scattering your attention and distracting you from what your right-hand column is trying to do. If, like Taylor, you're trying to communicate information, your left-hand column may bombard you with small but frantic doubts and preoccupations: *Do I sound garbled? Does that guy agree with me? Why does Sheila look bored out of her mind?*

Argyris noted that disciplined left-hand-column awareness can be an effective aid in communication, making you sensitive to how others are responding, and enriching the content of what you are trying to convey. And radar can enrich the content and accuracy of your right-hand column. But it's also easy to see how a well-developed radar can send your left-hand column out of whack. You may notice so many details that you lose track of what you're saying and why.

When this happens, your left-hand column becomes a source of absence rather than presence, a way of tuning out rather than tuning in. It becomes a source of weakness rather than a source of strength.

So how do you discipline your left-hand column so you can make it work in your favor?

Trying to suppress it is generally not a good idea. In fact,

Argyris cautioned that ignoring or blocking out left-hand thoughts was a good way to become a less effective and less intuitive communicator. That's because being out of touch with what you are actually thinking and feeling disconnects you from the people you're supposed to be engaged with. Your total absorption in your content comes off as robotic and inauthentic, which may make others wonder what you're trying to hide. In addition, suppressing what you notice consumes a lot of neural energy. So the effort can make you lose steam and feel exhausted.

For all these reasons, blocking out what you notice is not a good practice. Far better to manage your left-hand column so you can benefit from it without being overwhelmed.

REFRAMING

A great way to manage those pesky left-hand-column thoughts is to revise the story you tell yourself about what you notice. This is known as reframing. In essence, this is what Mirette advised Taylor to do.

Taylor says, "The observation that maybe the guy in the front row had just had a fight with his wife was one of the most helpful things anyone ever said to me. Now, whenever I find myself wondering why someone in a group or meeting seems irritated or distracted, I simply decide he's caught up with some personal problem or is reliving a disaster from his morning commute. Reframing the story I tell myself about what I notice helps me let go and focus on what *I* need to say without losing myself in my content."

Her apprehension at presenting in front of a large group made

Taylor forget that she frequently uses reframing in her own work with clients. "Say a client tells me he's 'not a people person.' I help identify examples of how he *does* connect with others so he can start telling himself a more helpful story and see himself in shades of gray instead of black and white. As a coach, I'm very familiar with Chris Argyris's theories. But when I found myself in a stressful situation, I got so hung up trying to read other people's reactions that I forgot how useful reframing could be."

Another way to reframe is to acknowledge what's in your left-hand column and find a way to work it into your right-hand column.

Hadley, who owns a garden design service, used this approach when the association she belongs to decided to honor her as a master in her field.

Hadley says, "I was very self-conscious about it. Even though our company has made some gorgeous gardens, I don't consider myself a master and I figured some of my colleagues would share that view. So I started reliving all the boneheaded things I'd done that should have disqualified me from being considered for the award."

Her mental preoccupation was such that, even as she tried to write a gracious and upbeat speech, Hadley's thoughts ran in the opposite direction. The conflict between what she was writing and what she was thinking made her feel like a fraud. As a result, she dreaded the event.

On the morning of the awards ceremony, Hadley read through her speech and immediately knew she had to set it aside. It was lovely, but it didn't reflect how she felt. So instead, she decided to go with her emotions and tell the audience about the doubts that being named a master had stirred up.

She says, "I didn't overplay the negatives or minimize my

achievements. But I did talk about my struggles and setbacks. I said that I didn't feel like a master, I felt like a beginner. That reminded me of the Buddhist concept of 'beginner's mind,' the idea that you should approach each task like a beginner so you don't get stuck on autopilot. As I said this, I realized that beginner's mind was one of the assets I brought to my work. It had probably kept me fresh for all these years. Making that discovery as I was speaking turned out to be pretty powerful."

The audience loved it. Sharing her vulnerability made Hadley seem real to them, and being honest felt right to her. But she could only do this when she stopped obsessing about how others might view her, and tell the truth as she saw it. When she finished, she received her first-ever standing ovation.

Reframing is powerful because it doesn't force you to choose between the thoughts racing through your mind and whatever it is you're actually trying to communicate. It enables you to access all the richness of your left-hand column without getting bogged down in the trap of either/or. By acknowledging what you're feeling and finding strength in that, you harness the power of your radar to banish its shadow side.

So the good news about overactive radar is that it's nothing more than a habit. It's not a deep characterological flaw. It's not a consequence of permanent neural wiring. It's not an unchangeable manifestation of who you are. Like the other eleven behaviors described in this book, it's a habit you can mitigate with the help of a few simple tools.

PART III

Changing for the Better

CHAPTER 17

Start with One Thing

S o now you know which habit—or, let's be honest, habits— may be playing a role in keeping you stuck. Maybe they're habits you've grown attached to because they helped you in the past. It's humbling to admit that what used to work for you has stopped working, and a little scary because familiar behaviors can feel like part of who you are. But it's inspiring to consider how much you might benefit from letting them go.

Here's the tough part: making sustainable and lasting change requires focus. Not just momentary "Let's do it" enthusiasm, but the willingness to make a consistent effort over time. This is best achieved by identifying one behavior, or even one *part* of one behavior, and working on it until you can see some progress. That's because making small changes, and repeating them until they become habitual, is more likely to yield long-term results than trying to become a brand-new you all at once.

You may have noticed this with dieting. Say you decide to stop having bread with your meals and then, a few weeks later, you cut out the cookies with your afternoon tea. If you stick with this gentle and minimal program, you will slowly but steadily lose weight. And you will probably keep it off by giving your system time to adapt to a minor change.

However, if you decide that, as of June 1, you're going to limit yourself to kale and seitan, you will probably lose weight fairly quickly. But after a few weeks, you'll find yourself cheating, which is the word people use when they don't want to admit they're going off their diet. Soon you'll cheat again, until you're back to rewarding yourself with ice cream. Then you'll set a new date for starting yet another brand-new-me program.

Do this a few times and you'll be a full-blown yo-yo dieter.

Yo-yo behavioral change operates similarly. It tends to fail over time because it relies entirely on willpower. But willpower is difficult to maintain over time. This isn't because you're weak or lazy, but because your brain is programmed to default to whatever requires the least effort and puts the least stress on your system. In practice, this translates as reverting to established habit.

By contrast, an incremental approach takes into account the powerful role of habit and default. That's because making small changes one at a time gives you the chance to practice each behavior until it becomes automatic. Once it no longer requires outsize effort, you can move on to another behavior if you choose to.

UNPACKING HABIT CLUSTERS

You've probably noticed that a number of the twelve habits described in the previous chapters have areas of overlap, or are to some degree a consequence of one another.

For example, if you have a problem with Habit 1, Reluctance

to Claim Your Achievements, you probably also struggle with Habit 2, Expecting Others to Spontaneously Notice and Reward Your Contributions. Both are rooted in the belief that "blowing your own horn" is obnoxious and reflect your fear of being perceived as "too ambitious." And both are conventionally viewed as nice-girl behaviors.

Maybe you're struggling with how to prioritize several overlapping habits you want to shake. That's not surprising, given that specific behaviors can form clusters or patterns, which makes them challenging to sort through. So let's look at some common habit clusters to see if any of them sound like you.

- If you identify with Habit 3, Overvaluing Expertise, you may also struggle with Habit 6, Putting Your Job Before Your Career. Both reflect a desire to keep your head down and focus on the task immediately before you instead of aiming at a larger long-term goal.
- These two behaviors often overlap with Habit 7, The Perfection Trap, since all three are rooted in the hope or expectation that you'll be rewarded if you just get every detail right. These habits often appear to others as a tendency to think small. They can result in your getting tagged as someone who'll willingly take on drudge work but isn't ready for the big-picture thinking that being a leader requires.
- Habits 9 and 10 also align, since both Minimizing and Too Much reflect a reluctance to speak your truth with clarity, intention, and force. Because you don't want to risk antagonizing others or making them feel bad, you may signal in advance that you're ambivalent about standing your ground. This can result in your being overlooked or disregarded.

- Habit 11, Ruminating, is often a consequence of Habit 12, Letting Your Radar Distract You. Because you notice so much, you have a lot to process and may end up mulling over negatives in a way that undermines you and keeps you stuck. This can make you appear disorganized or a bit clueless.

Once you identify the cluster of habits that's getting in your way, you can choose the one you want to tackle first. You'll find suggestions on how to overcome counterproductive behaviors in the next two chapters. But first, you'll need to figure out *where* to start.

BREAKING IT DOWN

A great way to start is by breaking down a problem behavior into discrete, specific habits that can be addressed one at a time. Say for example you recognize yourself in the description of Habit 8, The Disease to Please. Like Nancy, the hospital administrator profiled in Chapter 12, you think of yourself as helpful and giving and want others to see you this way. Your investment in your self-image leads you to dread saying no for fear of disappointing others. As a result, you routinely let your boundaries be violated and agree to requests you know you should turn down.

Maybe you decide to start addressing Habit 8 by pushing back on requests that don't serve your interests. But given that you've become accustomed to accommodating others, suddenly drawing a line in the sand feels arbitrary and categorical, the behavioral equivalent of switching to kale and seitan. So instead of going for overnight transformation, you might simply try to find out how much something actually matters to the person you're doing it for.

This was the approach taken by Miranda, the law firm associate profiled in Chapter 2, who volunteered to serve on her firm's recruitment committee just as her trial work was heating up. She quickly saw this was going to be a problem but didn't want to disappoint the colleague who'd recommended her for the committee. "I don't like disappointing people," she says. "That's not who I am. When someone asks me to do something, I try to deliver, even if it kills me."

Nevertheless she screwed up her courage and told her colleague about her misgivings. That's when he told her that he'd passed the invitation along to her because she "seemed like someone who would say yes." In other words, Miranda had tied herself up in knots trying to please a co-worker who had zero investment in her efforts. Having this information made it easier for Miranda to assert her boundaries.

There's a lesson here for anyone who identifies as a pleaser.

INTENTION SHAPES CHANGE

Miranda was able to identify a good first step to take because she saw that her need to please others was getting in the way of her litigation practice. This mattered a great deal to her, as she'd wanted to be a great trial lawyer since she was a child. Now that she was on the brink of starting to realize that ambition, she saw how her difficulty asserting boundaries could undermine the trajectory she was on. This gave her a powerful incentive to change a behavior that had previously served her.

Miranda's story demonstrates how having a clear understanding of what you are trying to achieve in life can be both a spur and a benefit when you seek to change. By contrast, Vera, the perfectionist profiled in Chapter 11, did not have this kind of incentive because she'd lost track of what she was really trying to achieve. Her avid attention to detail had served her until she was scouted for a senior executive position. Then, suddenly, it put her at a disadvantage. She knew this; the feedback she'd received from her coach and from colleagues was clear enough. But she couldn't let go of her habitual behavior because doing things perfectly had over time *become* her goal. She no longer knew what she was actually trying to achieve beyond proving herself to be the perfect person.

Like a number of behaviors described in this book, such as the need to please or overvaluing expertise, trying to be perfect can become a phantom that distracts you from your larger purpose. That's why knowing your purpose—defining it, speaking it, sharing it, and being intentional in its pursuit—can be a powerful asset as you address behaviors that undermine you.

So how do you become clear about your purpose?

You start by articulating concisely and precisely what you hope to achieve, either in your present job or over the long term. The idea is to clearly state the goal or purpose that most inspires you.

Your statement could be highly specific: You want to lead a global innovation team at a well-funded start-up. You want to be salesperson of the year in your company. You want to run for state office—and win. You want to head community outreach for your firm.

Your statement could also spell out a more general aspiration, what you see as your larger purpose in the world. Marshall has such a statement: *I help successful leaders achieve positive and last-*

ing change in behavior. Sally also has one: *I help women recognize their greatest strengths so they can act with confidence and intention.*

Once you have your statement, what do you do with it? You begin sharing it, over and over, in all kinds of situations, until your delivery becomes smooth and feels automatic. You keep it consistent but you refine it as you go along, trying to make it simpler and clearer.

Sally became aware of the power of articulating your purpose when working with Dong Lao, the executive sponsor of the women's initiative at a global financial institution described in Chapter 6. Delivering the keynote at the initiative's annual conference to six hundred women from around the world, Lao strongly urged everyone present to develop an "elevator speech" that reflected who they were and articulated what they wanted to achieve.

Lao based his advice on the statement of purpose he'd heard an ambitious young banker deliver in the literal elevator of the firm's London headquarters. It was brief, concise, thoroughly prepared, and designed to be rattled off at a moment's notice. The underlying message was clear: *This is what I do, this is what I intend to achieve. Keep your eye on me!*

A statement of purpose can also be useful when you're trying to identify which behavior you might benefit from addressing first. That's because articulating your purpose gives you a lens for deciding what may and what may not serve you as you work to accomplish the goal you've set for yourself.

For example, if your goal is to be a global ambassador for your company's brand, you'll probably want to address your reluctance to claim your achievements. That's because being a skilled megaphone for yourself will provide practice in becoming a skilled megaphone for your organization.

If your goal is to join your company's executive committee, you may want to address your habit of overvaluing expertise. That's because having a broad portfolio of responsibility will require you to become comfortable leaving the mastery of the details to others.

If you're fired by the desire to be the first female senior engineer in your company's most notoriously macho division, you may want to work on enlisting allies from day one. That's because you'll need behind-the-scenes advocates who can push back against doubts from higher-ups who don't know what you're capable of doing.

If you want to be recognized in your consulting firm as high potential, you may want to tackle your habit of minimizing. That's because routinely defaulting to phrases such as "I'm just trying to say," or "I only need a second of your time," or "it's like, ah..." signal that you're ambivalent about what you're trying to convey and aren't quite ready for a seat at the big table.

You get the idea. Tying your first step to your larger goal or purpose will give you a solid way to identify which behavior you might want to start with.

As you sort through your decision, it's helpful to keep in mind the old saying: *Perfect is the enemy of good.* In other words, don't agonize, don't imagine you need to start in the perfect place or get every step exactly right. Just get going.

CHAPTER 18

Don't Do It Alone

It's difficult enough to change a habit. But it's almost impossible to change it alone. Why? Because as humans, we all have a built-in forgetter. When we find ourselves in a familiar or triggering situation, we tend to default to our habitual response.

This is what operating on autopilot means. You don't have to think about what you're doing or put any effort into doing it, you just do it mindlessly, as you've always done it. You might remember afterward that you were trying to respond in a new, more constructive way. But in a moment of tension, stress, distraction, confusion, resentment, or simple overwork, you revert to your comfort zone.

Operating on autopilot *feels* efficient, and in many ways it is. If you had to consciously think through every turn of the wheel when you're driving, you'd never make it to work. If you had to decide where to put your foot every time you take a step, you'd falter when you tried to walk. Default serves you superbly when you're doing tasks that require repetition. But the ease of defaulting makes changing habits hard.

This is why coaching can be so useful. Coaches serve as

disruptors, reminding you that you're trying to change, and keeping your efforts on your front burner. A coach also acts as your partner as you seek to let go of habits that get in your way. Some of the women described in this book benefited from having coaches who offered feedback, disrupted familiar patterns, kept them on track, and held them accountable for new behaviors.

But what if you don't have a coach? After all, coaches can be expensive. And great coaches can be very expensive. Your company probably hires coaches only for its most senior executives. So if you're not at that level, working with a coach may be out of reach.

But it costs precisely nothing to enlist a colleague, friend, boss, or direct report in your effort to make positive behavioral changes. You just start by asking one person you trust for help in addressing a habit you would like to change. Involving someone else will disable your forgetter, make it harder to revert to autopilot, and make it harder for you to rationalize your resistance.

ENLISTING HELP

Say you decide that tackling the habit of pointlessly apologizing is a good place to start addressing your tendency to minimize. In this case, you could say something like this to a trusted colleague:

"Sharon, I'm wondering if you could help me out. I'm trying to be more effective in how I communicate but I've realized I'm in the habit of apologizing even when I've done nothing wrong. Sometimes I hear myself starting a simple observation with 'I'm sorry,' but most of the time I don't even notice. I'm wondering if you could let me know when you hear me say this since we'll be working together a lot over the next month. If other people are around, you could just nod or raise your eyebrows to cue me. I'd be grateful since this habit isn't helping me be my best."

Or say you decide you need to draw more attention to your achievements. Maybe like Ellen, the engineer in Chapter 2, you've gotten feedback from your boss that you need to be more proactive in helping him reach his goals. You realize he thinks this because you haven't kept him in the loop about what you're doing. So you ask a colleague who also attends your boss's weekly meetings to help you out.

You might say:

"Jim, since we sit next to each other in Jake's meetings, I'm wondering if I could enlist your help. I had a performance review last month, and one big takeaway was that I'm not letting Jake know all the things I'm doing to make our project more visible in the market. I'm guessing I need to be more assertive in meetings. Could you watch over the next few weeks and let me know if there's a way I'm underselling my contributions? I'd really appreciate your input."

Pulling others into your change efforts like this is not only more likely to make your new habits stick, it's also a great way to strengthen and deepen your relationships at work. Who doesn't like to be asked to share his opinions or observations? Who objects to being viewed as a trusted advisor whose insights and feedback are precisely what you need? The point is that enlisting the help of colleagues gives them a stake in your development. It demonstrates confidence in their judgment. It positions you as serious about your work. It may even inspire others to take similar action, which could help your whole team get better at what they do.

Of course, asking for help requires you to make yourself a bit vulnerable. This can feel awkward, because the default in most workplaces is to try to telegraph that you're in total control and don't need anyone's help. Given this, here are a few tips drawn from our experience that can reduce the discomfort or confusion you may feel.

1. *Choose carefully.* Ask for help from someone you trust, someone you have a good history with, and someone you know has a positive frame of mind. Since you'll be asking the person to observe you and give you feedback about a behavior, you'll also want to choose someone who sees you on a regular basis, either in meetings or as part of a team.

2. *Be specific.* Generalized requests won't get you the information you're seeking. Vague queries such as "do you think I'm doing well?" will put the person you're trying to enlist on the spot and leave too much room for subjective response. Instead, say precisely what you want her to notice, based on your start-with-one-thing template. This could be apologizing, oversharing, deflecting praise, underselling your achievements, minimizing body language, offering too much information, or trying to please too much—whatever behavior or habit you believe is getting in your way.

3. *Be concise.* Show the person you enlist that you value his time by making your requests as brief as possible. Avoid sharing a lot of background, providing long introductions, or repeating the same thing in different ways. And remember that being succinct requires you to prepare in advance. So know how you're going to phrase your request before

you make it, and think through how you can concisely respond to likely questions.

4. *Remember that disclosure is not the point.* Don't belabor *why* you want to change a habit or share your analysis of the reasons you behave as you do. It doesn't matter all that much to others. Keep in mind that you're seeking to change a behavior that limits your potential, not rehash the past or sign people up for a therapy session.

5. *Specify a time limit.* Don't ask for an open-ended commitment. Instead, request the person you engage to observe you at a specific event or for a bounded period of time, such as during a scheduled meeting or over the next few weeks.

How you ask for help is important. But it's not all that matters. You'll also want to be intentional about how you respond to the feedback you invite. You don't want to be reactive or appear upset if you hear painful truths, as this will make the person you enlist regret having signed on.

It's also good to have an advance plan for responding, especially as feedback is notoriously difficult to hear. Nobody enjoys being propositioned by a colleague or friend with the dread phrase "May I offer you some feedback?" You might smile, but you're probably gritting your teeth inside and holding yourself back from responding, *No, you most certainly may not.*

Unsolicited feedback feels like criticism, no matter how "helpfully" the observations are phrased, which is why it makes most people defensive. But when you enlist someone to offer their thoughts, you're soliciting the feedback, so defensiveness is beside the point and self-defeating.

Your task is to respond graciously and take what you need.

Marshall has developed a coaching template that provides guidance for using feedback when trying to change behaviors. It has four components: listening, thanking, following up, and advertising.

Listening

Simply listening to the feedback you receive is the first step, so you want to be sure you know how to listen. You might think, *of course I know how to listen, I'm a human being and I have ears.* But really listening to what someone else is saying requires discipline and focus. It also requires a measure of humility.

It's easy to forget in the heat of conversation that listening and speaking are two entirely different activities, which means you can't listen at the same time you speak. And you can't listen if you're preparing to speak—mentally rehearsing your response or champing at the bit to get your two cents in before the person you're supposed to be listening to is even finished.

When you do this, you may feel as if you're listening. But your mind is actually engaged with your own thoughts. Even if you manage to hear the words the other person is saying, you'll miss the nuances that are essential to real understanding.

And there's another problem: the person you're allegedly listening to knows when your thoughts are elsewhere because, try as you might, your body language gives you away. This is true even when you think you're doing a good impression of someone who's listening, nodding your head and saying *uh-huh* in all the right places.

But think about it. As we noted in Chapter 13, a small child can tell when your thoughts are elsewhere. So can your dog and your cat. Sentient creatures have a radar for detecting whether others are disengaged from what they are communicating. So how could a competent adult fail to notice?

Frances Hesselbein is one of the most skilled listeners we know. She practices listening as if it were an art form and is able to serenely take in information that might be upsetting or disturbing. She can do this because she understands that listening is always a two-step process. There's the part where you listen to what the other person has to say and then there's the part where you respond. They do not overlap.

Frances cites the late great Peter Drucker, her mentor and friend, as the best listener she ever knew. People he worked with hung on his every word. Yet he made it a practice to listen intently and fully before opening his mouth. In a meeting, he would ask everyone for an opinion before he offered his. "Peter," says Frances, "*always* went last." He wanted to take the temperature of what others were saying so he could gather all the information available. And he wanted time to formulate a thoughtful response.

How many leaders have you seen do this?

In most situations, the opposite happens. The most senior person present tries to assert dominance by being the first to respond, often cutting others off in the process. The message this sends is clear: *I'm more important than you are so I get to speak first. What I have to say is what really matters.*

Of course, the leader has every right to go first. But what is typically the result? Once the leader speaks, everyone else shuts down because nobody wants to contradict the most senior person. The upshot is that everyone falls into line without even expressing an opinion or sharing what might be vital information. This is the reason so many meetings feel pointless: they simply end up confirming the leader's already-held beliefs. By contrast, a leader who gives others the chance to speak first ends up surfacing new facts, unexpected perspectives, and fresh points of view.

So let's return to the situation where you've enlisted a colleague to observe a behavior you're trying to change. When the time comes for you to hear her observations, you want to do nothing but listen, which means keeping your ears open and your mouth shut. After all, you asked for her thoughts, so there's no reason to offer yours or explain or defend yourself. Even if you don't like what she's saying, even if it feels hurtful, even if you think she misinterpreted your concerns or missed the point, you want to respond to the feedback *you* solicited by listening to every word.

Thanking

And what do you do when the other person has finished speaking? You don't contradict, but you don't affirm, either. You don't offer your own opinion or rush to share an action plan. You simply say *thank you.*

Getting in the habit of thanking others is one of the most effective things you can do as you seek to rise. Like listening, thanking will help you at every stage of your career. That's because *thank you* works in almost any situation:

- It creates closure on difficult conversations.
- It stops the cycle of tit for tat.
- It's disarming—even people who are defensive soften when they are thanked.

- It makes others feel good and so increases the sum of happiness in the world.
- It demonstrates humility, showing you to be rightsized.
- Nobody can argue with it or push back.

Marshall advises all his clients to be radical fundamentalists when it comes to thanking. To be students and practitioners of gratitude and seek out opportunities to genuinely express it. To find ways to give themselves an A-plus in gratitude.

He does this because years ago he had the opportunity to experience the power of gratitude firsthand. Flying from Santa Barbara to San Francisco some years ago, he and his fellow passengers were informed by the crew that their landing gear had malfunctioned and they should prepare themselves for a crash.

During those frightening moments, Marshall asked himself what he most regretted in his life. The answer came clearly: he regretted not thanking all the people who had helped him or otherwise gone out of their way to be good to him. He resolved that, if he lived, he would seek out every one of those people and thank them.

The plane landed safely, and when he got to his hotel, Marshall immediately sat down and began writing sincere notes of appreciation to people who had helped him in his life, many of whom he hadn't been in touch with or even thought about for years. He continued to do this in the following months. His notes made the people who received them feel good, and writing them made him feel wonderful. The experience made him decide never to miss a chance to say thank you and to cultivate gratitude as a personal signature, a way of being in the world. And ever since, he's encouraged (that's putting it mildly) his clients to do the same.

Following up

Marshall and his colleague Howard Morgan studied outcomes from leadership development programs at eight major corporations to try to identify what people who succeed in making sustained positive behavioral changes have in common. They found the chief difference between those who were able to effect long-term change and those who were not lay in the amount of follow-up they did with colleagues. Results were consistent among participants in Europe, Latin America, North America, and Asia, indicating that the value of follow-up is universal.

What does it mean to follow up? It means that once you enlist someone's help, you keep them in the loop, ask how they think you're doing, make use of their suggestions, and tell them about it.

To see what this looks like, let's go back to the situation described earlier, where you realize you've failed to let your boss know how much you're contributing. You've asked your colleague Jim to observe you for a few weeks and share his thoughts about how you might be undercutting yourself.

When Jim gives you his feedback, he says he was surprised to notice that you often deflect credit for what you've achieved. For example, when your boss asked you in a meeting for an update on the status on a client initiative, you told him what everyone else on the team had done but never mentioned how you'd coordinated the service for your clients.

You listen intently to what Jim says. You don't interrupt or insert your thoughts but simply thank him for sharing what he noticed. And then the next time you're asked about your project in a meeting, you take his advice and describe exactly what you achieved. You call out team members who've been especially helpful and give credit where credit is due, but you do not try in any way to deflect it.

And then, once you've done all this, you follow up. This means asking Jim how he thinks you handled the meeting. After all, he's the one who noticed that you're in the habit of deflecting credit, so why not ask if he thinks you're doing better? Why not make him part of your development plan? Not by initiating a long conversation or sharing endless details, but by letting him know that you're acting on his ideas and by finding out if there's anything else he believes you could do to demonstrate a different kind of behavior.

Advertising

The fourth step is enlarging your circle of help beyond one or two people by doing what Marshall asks his coaching clients to do. You go all out in your effort by making everyone around you aware of how you're trying to modify or change a behavior that has gotten in your way.

This can be hugely effective because, as noted, people's perceptions of one another are notoriously slow to change. If you're seen as a reliable workhorse who won't necessarily fight for what she wants, one instance of standing up for yourself won't change that impression. If your comments are usually all over the place, people won't immediately notice when you're being more concise. If you've always kept your head down, people may not suddenly say to themselves, *I see Lucy is now really speaking up.*

So if you really want people to notice your commitment to changing a behavior, you'll want to articulate what you're doing at every opportunity, treating each day as a chance to drive home your message. Think of it as a publicity or election campaign, or a rolling press conference. Broadcast the message about your commitment to getting better.

This is what Maureen, the law firm partner profiled in Chapter 6, did after a male associate whose performance fell well short of hers was promoted and she was not. When a senior partner casually informed her that he had no idea she wanted to make partner because she'd never said so, she knew she had to change her approach. So she got busy telling everyone in the firm how set she was on this goal and what she was doing to make it happen.

She says, "It felt incredibly awkward and self-promoting, but I started telling people what I was doing, and also talking about what I needed to do to grow. I asked for ideas about how I could strengthen my skills and my position to better prepare for partnership. And I asked for feedback—*how'm I doing?* that sort of thing."

Her campaign at times felt like an extra burden, but Maureen was determined to position herself as a player who was unafraid to speak about her ambitions. This required her to present herself in a way that served her well once she did make partner: as a relentless advocate for what she believed in. In the end, she received the promotion that she wanted. Her only regret was that it took longer than it could have.

THE POWER OF PEER COACHING

If you really want to ramp up your change efforts, you might consider working with a peer coach. Both of us have taught peer coaching to clients, but we've also used it to change key behaviors ourselves.

Peer coaching takes the core principle of enlisting help and turns it into a semi-formal and ongoing process that is also recip-rocal instead of one-way. Basically, you commit to working regu-larly with a friend or colleague to hold one another accountable for specific behavioral changes you want to make.

You start by defining behaviors you want to work on, and break them down into specific actions. Then you schedule a regular time to report to one another on your progress.

When Marshall created his original template for peer coach-ing, he devised three simple criteria for choosing a peer coach.

Your peer coach should:

1. Be someone you enjoy touching base with regularly so it won't feel like a chore or burden. And your peer coach should feel the same way about you.
2. Have your best interests at heart. And you should feel the same about your peer coach.
3. Stick to the questions you prescribe and resist weighing in or making judgments. You should do the same for your peer coach.

That's it. Don't expect the magic to happen overnight. But if you work with your peer coach regularly, you will make positive changes consistently over time. You'll become better and you'll keep on getting better because your built-in forgetter will face disruption every day.

Marshall's personal practice is based on a simple list of ques-tions his peer coach asks him every night. He originally worked with a longtime friend and fellow coach, Jim Moore. Together they scheduled a phone call every evening, with no exception made for global travel.

As Jim's situation changed, Marshall shifted to working with other people. Over the years, he updated the items on his list to reflect his challenges in holding himself to account for becoming a healthier and better person.

Marshall's peer coach now asks him the following questions:

Did you set clear goals?
Did you make progress toward goal achievement?
Did you find meaning in what you did?
Were you happy?
Did you build positive relationships?
Were you fully engaged?
Were you patient?
Did you have a healthy diet?
Did you say or do something nice for Lyda (my wife)?
Did you say or do something nice for Bryan (my son)?
Did you say or do something nice for Kelly (my daughter)?
Did you say or do something nice for Avery and Austin (my grandchildren)?

This model has worked very well for Marshall. Since he travels constantly, his chief challenge is maintaining his health and good spirits and staying connected to the people he cares about. At times, Marshall has used a quantitative model, in which the questions can be answered with a number (for example, how many hours of sleep did you get?). But these days, it's more qualitative.

Sally's peer coaching template is a bit different, and has worked beautifully for her—so well that she's worked with the same peer coach for over eight years. Both she and Elizabeth Bailey, the long-time friend and fellow writer she enlisted, agree that touching base every day to review goals and behaviors has changed their lives.

Sally and Elizabeth connect by phone. They adjust their lists every few months, each targeting a specific theme for improvement. They devise five or six questions that relate to that theme and stick with the list until they can see solid progress on a desired behavior. Then they move on to something else.

The questions are rarely quantitative. They mostly focus on work and career goals, but usually include a few items that relate to personal growth. They use one another as a sounding board when deciding what issues to focus on. And sometimes they break Marshall's cardinal rule and offer suggestions: "Don't you think you might want to work on not being the perfect person next month?"

Here's a typical list that Sally used a couple of years ago. Her theme at the time was trying to be more visible as a speaker and writer. This is something she struggles with, as her tendency is to keep her head down and focus on her work instead of taking time to do the effective marketing that being a professional writer requires.

October–December 2016: Cultivating Visibility

1. Am I up-to-date with my website?
2. Did I check LinkedIn or send out a tweet?
3. Am I letting clients know what I'm up to?
4. Are my speaking topics current?
5. Did I spend time outdoors?
6. Was I grateful?

Sally worked from this list for several months, gradually swapping out specific items she acted on and adding other questions that related to her theme. Elizabeth did the same with her own list, and when each felt sure they had made real progress, they moved on to other challenges.

Both Marshall and Sally have found that addressing stubborn behaviors that hold them back is easier and more fun with a peer coach. That's why we recommend you make use of this powerful tool as you try to make incremental but positive behavioral changes.

Peer coaching works because it's the antithesis of doing it alone.

CHAPTER 19

Let Go of Judgment

You've identified a behavior that's been getting in your way. You have a clear idea of how you'll start working on it. You know whose help you're going to enlist. You know how you'll advertise that you're changing. You've got a plan for regular check-ins to measure your progress and keep yourself on track. Maybe you've decided to work with a peer coach.

You've also accepted that you'll hit a few bumps along the way. You understand that altering an ingrained behavior is difficult, usually a "two steps forward and one step back" proposition. But you're mentally prepared. And you're motivated because you're ready for a breakthrough. Or because you want to set a great example for your daughter. And because deep down you believe that, if more women like you become more influential, the world will be a better place.

So what do you need to look out for? What could set you back? In our experience, judgment is the number one thing that could get in your way. Judging yourself when you fall short of your expectations. Second-guessing what you're trying to do. Berating yourself because you're not making progress as quickly as you'd like. Regretting the habit you're trying to change now because it held you back in the past.

Critiquing yourself for every little thing.

Judgment can be a particular problem for women because women tend to be harder on themselves than men are. Yes, this is a generality, but in a combined six decades of working with leaders, Sally and Marshall found it to be true, and research involving leaders from around the world also supports it.

Women have some strong advantages when it comes to changing behaviors. For example, they tend to be less encumbered by ego than men, less defensive, and so more willing to seek and take advice. We rarely hear women say, "My real problem is that the people here are all jerks, so of course they're incapable of appreciating me." Or, "If everyone in this company would just suck it up and do what I say, we wouldn't have these problems."

Women's willingness to accept responsibility for their shortcomings can make them more open to correcting behaviors that hold them back and more diligent in how they go about changing established habits. But this admirable characteristic also has its downside. It means that women are less likely to give themselves a break or forgive themselves for the terrible sin of having an occasional flaw.

Judgment can trip you up when you're trying to change because it keeps you focused on the past instead of the present (see Habit 11, Ruminating). It's also negative and therefore inherently discouraging. That's why forgiveness and self-forgiveness are the most powerful tools we know for women with a tendency to judge or second-guess themselves.

Forgiving yourself usually starts with letting go of either/or thinking. Such as the belief that someone—you in this case—is either wonderful or terrible, a paragon or a disaster, perfect or a walking train wreck. And that making a mistake automatically tips you into terrible/disaster/train wreck territory. When you think about it, the either/or mind-set is unrealistic and a tad adolescent—as you may have noticed if you have teenagers, for whom everything is usually either great or terrible.

Either/or thinking also comes across as intolerant. And being intolerant with yourself will keep you stuck.

So if you have a tendency to self-judge, it's worth repeating that there is no ideal standard for humans in this world. Each one of us is a work in progress and will be until we draw our final breath. Accepting this, and being willing to embrace change while also letting go of judgment, is the most secure platform we know for achieving long-term positive change.

Feedforward

Okay, fine, you get that. But *how* do you let go of self-judgment? Especially if it's become a default or reflex?

One useful technique is feedforward, which Marshall has used for years with great success. You're already familiar with the basic concept, though not with the name, from the previous chapter because the basic ask/listen/thank template described there also applies to feedforward.

But what distinguishes feedforward from its familiar cousin feedback, and what makes it so useful for letting go of judgment, is that feedforward is concerned only with the future. With feedforward, you're not enlisting a trusted ally to observe you or send signals when you revert to a behavior you want to leave behind. Instead, you're simply requesting a few ideas you might use in the future. No critique or intervention is involved.

Say for example you've decided to work on distraction.

You've noticed your attention gets scattered whenever there's a lot going on or when you sense that people around you have conflicting agendas. Maybe you've also identified distraction as the root of your problem with Habit 6, Putting Your Job Before Your Career, since being overwhelmed by details makes it difficult for you to develop long-term plans. Or you've become aware that feeling distracted by what others might think is playing into your problem with Habit 8, The Disease to Please. Or you believe that if you could feel less distracted, you'd be able to communicate more concisely, and so make progress on Habit 10. The point is, because distraction can have many causes and manifestations, it's often a good place to start tackling a whole range of more complex behaviors.

Having made your decision, you approach a colleague or a friend and say something simple like: "I'm trying to work on becoming less distracted so I can focus on one thing at a time. Do you have any ideas I could use? Any practices that have worked for you?"

Perhaps you'll hear something like, "Yeah. I often find meetings distracting because there's so much going on. So I try to write down exactly what I want to learn ahead of time and keep my attention on that. Why don't you try it?"

Your job when soliciting comments like these is simply to listen to what the person says. You don't want to offer any response except a gracious *thank you*. No commentary, objection, or agreement. No "what a great idea, I'm going to try that tomorrow." And certainly no "that would never work for me because..." You're just soliciting ideas.

A great thing about feedforward is that you don't have to be choosy about who you ask. You're not requesting that the person observe or critique you. You're not enlisting a peer coach or asking to be held to account for changing a behavior. Because you're not making yourself particularly vulnerable or inviting scrutiny, you don't need to choose someone you deeply trust or who you know has your best interests at heart. After all, you're just looking for suggestions.

Since inviting feedforward is no big deal, you can feel free to ask a lot of people and get a whole lot of suggestions. That's great, the more the merrier, because you're under no obligation to take any of them. Meanwhile, you're informing people about what you're trying to do, how you're trying to change for the better. This makes it more likely that they'll notice you're improving. So feedforward can serve as a kind of positive advertising.

A final advantage of feedforward is that it's a lot less fraught than feedback. It doesn't feel personal like feedback does. As noted, most of us shrink in dread when someone says, "Can I offer you some feedback?" We mentally arm to defend ourselves from an attack. But you have to be a pretty sensitive plant to shrink from hearing a few suggestions about how you might handle a challenge in the future.

So if self-forgiveness is a problem for you, try using feedforward. It's one of a number of exercises that can help you let go of judgment.

OH WELL

Another powerful technique is laughably simple. It's learning to say *oh well*. As in: *Oh well, I messed up. Oh well, I'm not perfect. Oh well, someone misinterpreted what I meant to say.*

Oh well signals self-acceptance, a recognition that you're only human and that as a human you sometimes make mistakes. It's the opposite of, *OMG, how could I have done that? How could I have said that? What must she/he think? I'm such a dolt! Will I never learn?*

Oh well also signals that you're ready to move on. No wallowing in regret. You just acknowledge that you made a mistake and turn your attention to what you can do next.

Oh well is a neat little habit of Marshall's that Sally picked up while working with him on this book. It's not an exercise he does with clients or in workshops. It's just something he models every day.

Spending time with Marshall, Sally heard it a lot. *Oh well, I missed that call I was supposed to be here for.* Or *Oh well, I forgot that guy's name.* Hearing this was enormously helpful because Sally often has a hard time forgiving herself for the kind of normal human errors that any busy person inevitably makes.

In addition to being hard on herself, Sally tends to hang on to past mistakes for years. *How about that time I forgot to ask my client about her daughter's wedding, which she'd been talking about for the last four years? How about that time I gave a talk to people who I thought were in HR but they were actually in communications? How about when I was dehydrated from travel and delivered that shaky performance at a high-stakes workshop? How could I have messed up so badly? What's wrong with me?*

This is a long-established habit, so Sally barely noticed that *oh well* was having a subtle influence on her until one morning, when she found herself in the kind of situation that would usually have triggered a tailspin.

She received an e-mail before 7 a.m. from the editor of an arti-

cle she'd written that had been posted online the previous evening. Five minutes after the posting, the subject of her interview
had e-mailed the editor to let her know that Sally had misidenti-
fied his birthplace.

Sally's first impulse was to slide into self-recrimination: *I've
been a writer for decades, how could I have gotten something so basic
wrong? I'll lose credibility with the magazine and never be assigned a
major profile again. And the guy I wrote about must think I'm a total
amateur. This is a disaster!*

But after about two minutes of stewing, the words came into
Sally's mind fully formed: *Oh well! Oh well, so I got one detail
wrong. Oh well, it was an honest mistake. And oh well, the story
hasn't been published in the print edition yet so it can be corrected.*

She contacted the subject of the article, got a quick response,
and sent the editor the correct information. Ten minutes later, the
change had been made. Yes, she had made a mistake. But it qualified as a glitch, not a disaster.

Oh well!

For the rest of the week, Sally made *oh well* her mantra. She
printed out a banner in 40-point font and hung it above her desk.
And she shared it with her husband, Bart. He's an artist and quite
sensitive to people and their reactions, so he's prone to ruminating
about micro-situations he thinks he should have handled better,
unlike a lot of the men Sally works with, who seem more resistant
to giving themselves a hard time.

Bart loved it. And the next morning, when Sally went into
his home office to pick up the phone, she found a big reminder
scrawled on the bulletin board above his desk. In giant letters he
had written: OH WELL!

LEAVE IT IN THE STREAM

Marshall often illustrates the futility of holding on to past judgments with a favorite Buddhist parable. It appears in the original *What Got You Here Won't Get You There*, but it also applies here.

Two monks were strolling by a stream on their way home to the monastery when they were startled by the sound of a young woman in a bridal gown sitting by the stream, crying softly. Tears rolled down her cheeks as she gazed across the water. She needed to cross to get to her wedding, but she feared that doing so would ruin her beautiful handmade gown.

In this particular sect, monks were prohibited from touching women. But one monk was filled with compassion for the bride. Ignoring the sanction, he hoisted her on his shoulders and carried her across the stream, assisting her on her journey and saving her gown. She smiled and bowed with gratitude as the monk splashed back across the stream to return to his companion.

But the second monk was livid. "How could you do that?" he scolded. "You know we are forbidden to touch a woman, much less pick one up and carry her around!"

The offending monk listened in silence to a stern lecture that lasted all the way back to the monastery. His mind wandered as he felt the warm sunshine and listened to the singing birds. Once home, he fell asleep for a few hours but was jostled awake in the middle of the night by his fellow monk.

"How could you carry that woman?" his friend demanded again. "Someone else could have helped her. You're a bad monk!"

"What woman?" the sleepy monk inquired.

"Don't you even remember? That woman you carried across the stream."

"Oh, her," laughed the sleepy monk. "I only carried her across the stream. You carried her all the way back to the monastery."

The learning point here is simple. When you make a mistake or otherwise find yourself behaving like a human, the best practice is to *leave it at the stream*. Don't carry it around like that angry monk who kept obsessing about the other monk's behavior. Just lay that burden down and let it go.

THE TO-DON'T LIST

You probably have a daily to-do list full of tasks, commitments, and intentions—things you must get done or would like to accomplish. Maybe you check off items one-by-one as you go through your day, which gives you a sense of accomplishment and satisfaction. Maybe you like to look back on your lists because they offer proof in black and white that you haven't wasted your time and demonstrate the progress you're making on your goals.

To-do lists help you stay organized and efficient. They're useful tools, even if sometimes you wake up feeling as if your to-do list runs your life. As if you're merely an instrument whose chief purpose is meeting the demands your list imposes.

As you move higher, your to-do list usually becomes longer, and the tasks involve higher stakes. Certainly *Approach finance committee chair about new strategic plan* has a greater weight than *Submit expenses for client lunch*.

But as your list expands and feels more urgent, you might

want to also consider a to-don't list, a list of items you would like to let go of. These could include things you want to stop doing and tasks you want to drop or hand off. By identifying activities that eat up your time, keep you trapped, or offer minimal reward, a to-don't list brings intentionality to what you want to say no to.

In her workshops for women leaders, Sally defines being intentional as *knowing what to embrace and what to let go of as you move to a higher level.* The embrace is the to-do list. The let go of is the to-don't list. Balancing them requires you to give conscious attention to how you manage responsibilities, relationships, and behaviors so you can decide what really matters and what does not.

If instead you just keep adding tasks to your to-do list, you'll start to feel overwhelmed as you rise and take on more responsibility. If this happens, you may end up strip-mining your inner resources, making it impossible to operate in a way that is sustainable, energizing, and enjoyable. And one day you'll wake up and say, *What's the point?*

Items on your to-don't list can be big or small, but your list will be most effective if it describes specific actions rather than attitudes, aspirations, or complex behaviors. This will make it manageable and concrete and provide you with items you can check off as you move through your day.

Here are some examples from women who have participated in Sally's workshops:

- I will let go of answering the phone on the first ring—it makes me feel rushed and doesn't give me time to prepare.
- I will let go of immediately saying yes or no to requests so I can take time to think about what works for me.

- I will let go of nodding my head when someone's talking because I've learned that this often gets interpreted as assent or agreement.
- I will let go of trying to win the regard of my colleague because she's made it clear that she resents me.
- I will let go of getting pulled into the gossip fests that plague our unit.
- I will let go of answering questions with *Yes but*, since it's just a disguised way of contradicting others.

Jeri, a communications consultant from Denver, describes the workshop in which she did this exercise as a turning point in her career. She says: "As my business expanded, I kept adding things to do—every day, every week, every year. It started to feel oppressive, as if I were some kind of victim, as if the business I'd dreamed of running was running me. Creating a to-don't list, and holding myself accountable for letting things go, gave me a way out of this swamp. Now I'm constantly on the lookout for things I can *not* do, whether it's scheduling extra staff meetings or packing lunches for everyone at my son's baseball practice. If I decide something's not really important, and won't add real benefit to the day, I simply say, *Sorry, but that's on my to-don't list.*

JUDGING OTHERS

If you're in the habit of judging yourself, you may also be in the habit of judging others. After all, since you're always pushing yourself to meet the highest possible standards, why would you give other people a break?

So if you've decided to let go of self-judgment using the tools described above, you might also consider letting go of judging others as well. Your load will get lighter if you leave your judgments in the stream instead of carrying everyone's behaviors around with you.

This can be countercultural in a lot of organizations, where people jockey for position (subtly or not) by zestfully enumerating their colleagues' failings. It's extraordinary when you consider how many hours of time are consumed and how much productivity is lost in the endless recounting of co-worker blunders, and how much stress is created by reliving real or imagined slights.

If this all-too-typical time suck afflicts you or your team, you can benefit by simply withdrawing from participation. You can jump off the gossip wagon and just refuse to go there. Declining to focus on what others get wrong can give you a big boost when you're trying to initiate behavioral changes or break established habits that have kept you stuck. Instead, you turn your attention to what's positive and what lies within your control.

Minding your own behavior is also helpful in avoiding a common trap you may fall into when trying to change: expecting others to be wowed by how much you're improving. The fact is, this probably won't happen for the simple reason that most people have a lot going on and are focused on themselves. So they're unlikely to offer kudos when you let go of an outgrown habit, even if it's a habit they found irritating in the past. Your best bet is to draw their attention to it, maybe using feedforward or another advertising technique, and then move on. Keep your attention on what you can change—which is basically yourself.

Another judgment pitfall you may encounter when trying to

change a behavior is unconsciously expecting that others will change along with you. But unless they've committed to a major personal improvement program, it's doubtful that, just because you're getting better, everyone around you will start becoming more wonderful too. So resist questioning why your colleague seems so tongue-tied in the meeting and then feels bad when her contributions get overlooked. You may be a paragon of self-advocacy now, but a few months ago you may have behaved a lot like her.

Either/or thinking is often at fault when you find yourself judging others, just as it is when you're overly critical of yourself. Either your team is composed of fabulous people who adore you and always get the job done, or they're a bunch of mediocrities who inevitably disappoint. When you hear yourself voicing such views, or even just giving them space in your thoughts, you might want to remind yourself that either/or expectations can lead you to trust the wrong people, or not trust the people you should. Why? Because putting others in extreme categories inevitably clouds your judgment.

While you're reexamining these attitudes, you might also want to jettison your critique of how "political" your colleagues and bosses are, often and especially including the men. Yes, your peer clapped wildly when the boss introduced a new initiative in the quality meeting, even though he had been trashing the same idea the previous week. But instead of deciding the guy's a hypocrite who's playing the typical hierarchical game, why not consider that he's just a working stiff with a family to support who's doing what he believes he must to stay employed? It's not surprising that this includes flattering a boss who has repeatedly made it clear he's a sucker for even the most flagrant brownnosing.

Judging others often finds expression in phrases such as, "You'd think someone who has reached his level would be more thoughtful." Or "You wouldn't expect a managing partner to act like such a jerk."

The question you might want to ask yourself if you hear these words fall from your lips is simply *why*? What exactly in the history of the world, or the history of organizations, supports the idea that powerful leaders are always good-hearted and enlightened persons who routinely treat others with respect and make great decisions?

Yes, outstanding leaders have an outsize impact, and we are fortunate when we work with such people. But they are rare. So it doesn't make much sense to expect that, just because someone reaches a high position, he or she *would* (fill in the blank).

The problem with judgment is that it gets in your way, sucks up your time, and makes positive change more difficult. It also demonstrates ill will to your fellows, which inevitably comes through, even when you think you're cleverly disguising your assessment.

Judgment of self or of others won't improve the quality of your life. It certainly won't make you happier. But it will keep you stuck when you're trying to shift behaviors so you can become that most wondrous of creatures, your best self.

CHAPTER 20

Remember What Got You Here

Successful women tend to be avid self-improvers. You probably are, since you're reading this book. One of the many reasons we enjoy working with successful women on habits and behaviors that get in their way is that they rarely react defensively to suggestions about how they could get better. On the contrary, they usually listen attentively and then set to work with enthusiasm and zest.

Marshall's story about working with Frances Hesselbein in Chapter 1 is an example. Frances is one of the leaders Marshall admires most in the world. Her accolades, worldwide honors, and extraordinary range of close connections make clear that she's a master when it comes to relationships and leadership skills.

Yet when Marshall delivered a 360-degree feedback assessment to Frances at her request, her immediate response was to focus on what she needed to improve. No lecture on how fabulous she was or how great her results were, as male leaders are more likely to deliver. Frances was in fact so eager to start making changes that Marshall realized his biggest challenge in coaching her would be persuading her to be less self-critical.

You may share this passion for improvement with Frances. If so, it's important to bear in mind that every limiting behavior is also rooted in a strength. Your strengths are what got you here, here being where you are now. They may not get you there—that is, where you want to go. But you will benefit from maintaining a healthy respect for the gifts you bring and for what you have achieved as you go about addressing behaviors that may have limited you in the past.

For example, it's helpful to recognize that:

Habit 1, Reluctance to Claim Your Achievements, is rooted in genuine modesty and a generous willingness to acknowledge the achievements of others.

Habit 2, Expecting Others to Spontaneously Notice and Reward Your Contributions, is rooted in a reluctance to showboat or behave like a self-promoting jerk—along with the perception that, because *you* notice what others contribute, other people will (or should) too.

Habit 3, Overvaluing Expertise, is rooted in a healthy respect for all the skills your job requires and the willingness to work hard to master them.

Habit 4, Building Rather Than Leveraging Relationships, is rooted in the conviction that you should value others for who they are rather than how they can be of use to you.

Habit 5, Failing to Enlist Allies from Day One, is rooted in the belief that you should not call on others for help until you've done your homework and know the parameters of your job.

Habit 6, Putting Your Job Before Your Career, is rooted in the desire to demonstrate loyalty and commitment, as well as the sensible belief that you should take life one step at a time instead of getting all wrapped up in the future.

Habit 7, The Perfection Trap, is rooted in the desire not to disappoint others (including and perhaps especially your family of origin), along with a commitment to making the world a better place.

Habit 8, The Disease to Please, is rooted in an unselfish passion for making other people happy.

Habit 9, Minimizing, is rooted in an awareness of other people's needs and the wish to show them that you value their presence and insights.

Habit 10, Too Much, is rooted in the quest to be authentic and connect with others based on shared experience.

Habit 11, Ruminating, is rooted in the capacity for thinking deeply about what matters most to you instead of skimming along the surface of your life.

Habit 12, Letting Your Radar Distract You, is rooted in the ability to understand what others are feeling and a broad-scale noticing capacity that makes you intuitive and empathic.

You see the pattern here. Certain characteristics emerge: diligence, conscientiousness, a concern for the feelings and contributions of others, and a reluctance to join the it's-all-about-me competition that characterizes life and politics in many organizations.

These are good things. They are gifts you bring to the world. And they surely have contributed to your success. And since part of your success will ultimately be helping to make your organization, and the world, a better place, you don't want to leave these strengths behind as you move higher and expand your scope.

Nevertheless, fulfilling your potential is bound to take you beyond your comfort zone, and examining how your strengths may also undermine you is one aspect of that. That's why you'll want to celebrate the skills, talents, attitudes, and behaviors that have brought you to where you are. Even as you identify and work to surmount self-limiting behaviors that won't get you where you want to go.

We believe that far more women could and should be in positions of power and influence. We hope that our ideas will ultimately help you rise in your chosen field or organization so you can make even more of a positive difference in the world.

Acknowledgments

Sally and Marshall gratefully acknowledge:
One another—friends and colleagues for 25 years
Mike Dulworth—who gave us the idea for this book
Jim Levine—who signed on as agent in 30 seconds
Mauro DiPreta—who saw the possibilities
Michelle Howry—our wonderful editor
The stellar sales and marketing team at Hachette
Elizabeth Bailey—Sally's peer coach
Alan Mulally—Marshall's role model

Index

About the Authors

Sally Helgesen has been recognized as one of the world's top experts on women's leadership for almost thirty years. As an author, speaker, and consultant, her mission has always been to help women recognize, articulate, and act on their greatest strengths.

Her best-selling *The Female Advantage: Women's Ways of Leadership*, hailed as "the classic work" on women's leadership styles and continuously in print for twenty-eight years, was the first book to focus on what women have to contribute to their organizations rather than how they need to change and adapt. *The Web of Inclusion: A New Architecture for Building Great Organizations* was cited in the *Wall Street Journal* as one of the best books on leadership of all time. Most recently, *The Female Vision: Women's Real Power at Work* explored how women's strategic insights can strengthen their careers and benefit their organizations.

Sally develops and delivers leadership programs for corporations, partnership firms, universities, and associations around the world. She has consulted with the United Nations on building more inclusive country offices in Africa and Asia, led seminars at the Harvard Graduate School of Education and Smith College, and is a contributing editor to *Strategy + Business* magazine. She lives in Chatham, New York.

Marshall Goldsmith is the world authority in helping successful leaders achieve positive, lasting change in behavior. He is the only person to have been recognized twice as the *Thinkers50* World's Most Influential Leadership Thinker. Marshall has been frequently listed as the World's Top Executive Coach. In 2017, he was recognized at Harvard as the inaugural winner of the Leadership in the Field of Coaching Award by the Institute of Coaching.

Marshall is the *New York Times* #1 best-selling author of *Triggers* and *What Got You Here Won't Get You There,* both recognized by Amazon.com as two of the one hundred best books ever written on leadership and success. His many books have sold more than two million copies and have been translated into thirty-two languages.

He is one of a select few executives who have been asked to advise more than 150 major CEOs and their management teams. Marshall lives in Rancho Santa Fe, California, and New York City.

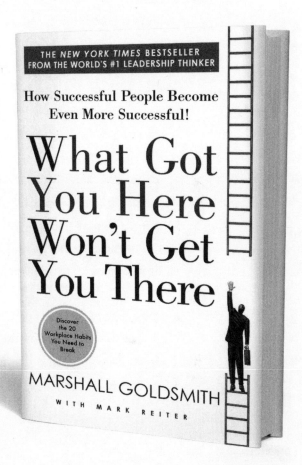